BOOK ENDORSEMENTS

If you're looking for a pithy and practical approach to real prosperity, this is it! Greg is more than an author, he's the real deal; a role model who practices what he teaches. The book accomplishes all that it says and then some. It is reader-friendly and well structured. After introducing the vision (Chapter 3), Greg gives you six compelling steps to make that vision a reality (Chapter 4). And then six more steps (Chapter 7) to keep you FREE!

I've had the pleasure of working with Greg and serving on a board with him, and what he brings to the table is a banquet of ideas that you can feast on for long after you're out of his presence. And if the book isn't enough, the CD that comes with the book, makes this purchase a no-brainer: a wise investment!

There is no social security in the government, if you understand the concept properly. Our "true security" is in applying and living the Biblical principles right here in your hands. No more excuses: Just Do It!" II Corinthians. 9:6

– Ernie Fitzpatrick, Senior Pastor, Liberty Revival Church

Greg Petsch is the Tom Landry of finances. Within these pages you will discover the principles, the practical steps and tools for you to be a champion over your money.

Becoming wealthy does not require you to know some hidden secretive formula that is out of your reach, reserved only for the rich. Instead, Greg reveals that anyone can be wealthy - it only takes courage, discipline and applying the values imbedded in this book.

I know this to be true from my own personal experience of debt reduction over these past few years. I also have had the privilege to hear the testimonies of many from my church that are now debt free and building wealth from these timeless truths. This is not your typical "get out of debt" book. I believe this book is a classic and over time it will be recognized as such.

– Dr. Ron Rhea, Pastor, LifeSprings Christian Church

I have known Greg as a man of integrity, vision and determination for almost twenty years, and been privileged to teach with him for eleven of those twenty years. To me and many he has helped catch a new vision, Greg is a General in the "War on Debt." This book, *Debt, You're Fired, Wealth You're Hired* gives us a weapon, a battle plan to defeat debt, so we can become the generation to "rebuild the walls "around our Jerusalem and take back the land our enemy has taken. All of the tools necessary to defeat your Goliath and take your place as a financial leader in your family, your church, your community, and the body of Christ are laid out for you in this book. I pray that as you read this book you will catch the passion contained in these pages for living your financial life for God, and then go and infect all you encounter with the same passion.

– Rick A Watts III, President, Geoscience Solutions, Inc.

Greg Petsch has a unique call of God on his life that possesses a very credible anointing and passion to help people defeat debt. Although God has blessed Greg with great success, he walks in humility, compassion, and uncompromising integrity.

In *Debt, You're Fired, Wealth You're Hired* he challenges the reader to create a desire and expectancy to break free from debt. This book is not only an instructional manual, but also contains the tools to assimilate a debt elimination plan.

Debt, You're Fired, Wealth You're Hired provides the knowledge, inspiration, and encouragement to empower you to defeat debt. It will guide you to establish realistic goals and enable you to dream again.

– Bruce P. McGaugh, Investment Consultant, Sr. Vice President, RBC Dain Rauscher

Debt, You're Fired, Wealth You're Hired was counterintuitive to me. After 40 years as a salesman and sales manager it was our hope that our sales people were always hungry. Theory was that everyone would sell more if they lived beyond their means. Well, that was another era - another time. A time when companies offered retirement plans that were there when you needed them. 401k's could be counted on for your golden years. Today, we've learned you can't count on these vehicles. You need do your own planning for your own future. Greg Petsch has written a book for modern times. The savvy person keeps his options open by creating and following a plan to be debt free. God's hand will guide you on your path to freedom.

– Ross Cooley - retired, Former Chairman/ CEO pc-order.com and Sr. Vice President/ General Manager North America Sales, Compaq Computer Corporation

John 10:10 says "…I am come that they might have life, and that they might have it more abundantly." Imagine a life free of financial bondage. Financial freedom enables God's people to invest energy in the true purpose that He has for each of us.

Debt, You're Fired, Wealth You're Hired is a must-read for those interested in building wealth God's way. Greg Petsch shares with readers biblical principles that support his ideas on how to build wealth, and he includes a Spending Plan CD which reinforces the concepts in his book. The package is a great value for people of all ages.

– Dr. Eli Jones, Professor, Writer, Teacher

Greg Petsch has now provided a practical, experience proven guide complete with a simple to use financial planning CD that can be personalized to meet your needs to eliminate debt and build wealth.

This is must reading for anyone that has tried to stop the debt cycle only to return to the burden of debt. In *Debt, You're Fired, Wealth You're Hired*, there is realistic, hands-on assistance for everyone regardless of where you are in the process of debt elimination and wealth building. Greg reminds us that it doesn't matter where you have been; it is where you are going that will determine your success.

Before reading the book, I had conflict whether or not the personal planning and achievement of financial goals could really support God's plan for me. Greg has provided in his book a Biblical based perspective regarding the tithe, offerings, and the building of wealth as God's steward free of guilt.

Greg Petsch is a fine man devoted to God and family, committed to fulfill God's purpose for him during his time on earth. I have been blessed to have known Greg for over 20 years and worked with him for over 15 of those years.

– Charlie Winder, Senior Vice President, Quanta Computer Inc.

Greg Petsch has one of the most thorough and balanced understandings of Biblical prosperity of anyone I know. This book will help you not only understand the principles, but aid you in applying them to your life. As part of the pastoral team at Lakewood Church, I have personally seen how Greg's direct counsel and debt-retiring plans have freed people of millions of dollars of debt. I wholeheartedly recommend you read this book as it will help you find the right path to debt free living.

– Marcos Witt, Pastor Lakewood Church, Spanish Church

Debt, You're Fired, Wealth You're Hired establishes a sound biblical foundation for changing your mind in order to get on the path to prosperity. The genius of this book goes beyond changing the way you think and provides a practical, step by step plan for making it happen. Over the years I have counseled many people on how to get control of their finances and become a steward of God's provision. From now on I will start by handing them this book as required reading. I wholeheartedly recommend this book as a roadmap for anyone who is serious about changing their financial future and their life for the better.

– Paul J. Sarvadi, Chairman, CEO, Administaff, Inc.

Every bookstore is overrun with "self-help" books. There are secular "self-help" books on financial planning and strategies as well as Christian "self-help" books on living a Godly life following biblical principles. The uniqueness of *Debt, You're Fired, Wealth You're Hired* is Greg Petschs' use of biblical principles in teaching us to plan, avoid debt, and create wealth.

I serve on a board with Greg and I am fortunate to know him personally. I can say without equivocation that there is not a more sincere man of God, nor a more sanguine financial thinker. I know this is a book of love and dedication for Greg where he shares Biblical truths which have affected his personal, financial, and spiritual life. It is a "must read" for all families.

– Jack Fields, Former Member of Congress (1980-1996), Texas' Eighth Congressional District

If teenagers and college students would gain an understanding of the impact that compounded growth would have on their lives (chapter 7), there would be many more millionaires in the United States! This book is a real, Biblical "How To" on getting rid of debt and gaining wealth. Greg's insight gives easy and practical solutions on how to systematically make debt a thing of the past. Act now with patience and perseverance; and the Jones' will wish they had bought this book!

– Danny Watterson, Student Pastor, Lakewood Church, Houston, Tx

DEBT
YOU'RE
FIRED
Wealth
YOU'RE
HIRED

Positioning Yourself For
Biblical Prosperity

GREG E.
PETSCH

Library of Congress Cataloging-in-Publication Data

Petsch, Greg E. 1950 -
Debt, you're fired – positioning yourself for Biblical prosperity / Greg E. Petsch.

p.cm.
Includes bibliographical references.
ISBN 0-9785141-0-6 (paperback)
1. Personal finance. 2. religious. 3. 1. Title:
Debt, you're fired, wealth, you're hired II. Title.

Printed in the United States of America.

DEDICATION

A wife of noble character is the crown of her husband.
— *Proverbs 12:4*

I would like to dedicate this book to my wife and best friend, Carla. She is certainly a gift from God who has lived her life as a Proverbs 31 woman of God.

She has given of herself to not only become an excellent wife but an outstanding mother and grandmother. She has been my support throughout our marriage. Carla operates with the gift of helps. She is the one that is in the background working, never seeking the spotlight. She knows her rewards come from God above and seeks his best for our family. She provides a balance for me in life and has made my life happier than I imagined from that day on June 19, 1971 when our marriage covenant occurred.

I also dedicated this book to God the Father, His son Jesus and the Holy Spirit. He has entrusted me to be a steward for Him and it is my desire to pass onto you, in this book, some of the wisdom He has given me in life. I am of the belief; this book can change people's lives. You can financially become a testimony and not a statistic. Set your mind towards victory!

TABLE OF CONTENTS

FOREWORD

Greg has a passion to let people know that God's plan is for their financial freedom, not slavery to debt. In *Debt, You're Fired, Wealth You're Hired,* Greg paints a vision of financial freedom for the reader, and gives practical tools to make the vision become reality!

Over the last 4 years, Greg has helped hundreds of people at Lakewood Church (Houston, TX) realize their dream of financial freedom. The comments we hear are overwhelming – "I never thought it was possible! For the first time, I have hope."

I've heard it said, "If you want something to be different in your life, you have to do something differently." *Debt, You're Fired, Wealth You're Hired* is the "something different." I challenge every person struggling under the burden of debt to invest in a copy of this book. Let the Holy Spirit create a vision in your heart for financial freedom, and as you put into practice the action steps Greg has outlined, I am confident you will walk in the abundant life that God has planned for you!

– Paul Osteen, M.D.

ACKNOWLEDGEMENTS

The idea for this book began in my spirit in the mid 1990's. I have been given the opportunity to teach Biblical economics in many churches. I also have ministered God's Word on finances in several countries. After developing a process to teach people how to become the lender and not the borrower, I was encouraged by Kristin Anderson in 2005. She began the Debt, You're Fired process in her personal life and became passionate about getting her financial house in order. Through her encouragement and perseverance I began to write this book. It is my prayer you will become as passionate about your debt firing plan as Kristin is.

I would also like to thank my God's Money Man financial ministry team; Rick Watts and Bruce McGaugh. Rick and I have taught Biblical Economics together since 1995. He has been a living example of God's plans in people's lives in the area of discipline and process. Rick taught me about God's covenant and continues to co-teach with me. Bruce joined our team in the late 1990's and is also a God's Money Man team co-teacher. Bruce lives the Proverbs 10:22 life and is an example of Godly stewardship and giving. These men have become great friends and supporters of this financial ministry. I am grateful that God brought them into my life.

Thanks and appreciation to Dr. Paul Osteen. In 2002, Dr. Paul had a vision to create a financial ministry at Lakewood Church in Houston, Texas. He reviewed our God's Money Man program and materials, and allowed me to implement the seminars and individual spending plans at our church. Dr. Paul has been an advocate of getting people out of debt and into the financial freedom as it is written in the Bible.

Many thanks to the Financial Biblical Coaches (FBCs). They have caught the vision of God's Money Man. They have become trained to work individually with people to create a spending plan, using the software included in this book. All of the FBCs volunteer to use their life experiences to teach others how to become the lender and not the borrower.

In early 2002, I met Dr. Ron Rhea. He is pastor of Life Springs Christian Church in Leander, Texas, a small town northwest of Austin. Pastor Ron has been a model for pastors to use to implement a Biblically-based financial teaching and application process successfully in his church. He has a group of believers at Life Springs that have become connected to the church's vision. On March 20, 2005, the church's mortgage was burned and Life Springs became a debt-free church.

I also owe a debt of gratitude to my mother and father. Wally and Ava Petsch raised seven children. Through their teaching me about money, discipline, and love, I was prepared to become the person I am today. Many mornings at 4 am, Mom was there helping me fold newspapers. Mom was always there when you needed her. Dad was an accountant. He taught me how to manage money and invest it. They also set the example for me by never paying interest on a credit card.

Last, and definitely not least, my gratitude goes to my wife Carla, and daughters Kristina and Brandi. While I talk about debt and money extensively in this book, I understand that prosperity is far greater than just money. I am a prosperous man even if I did not have a dollar, because God has given me my family. Please understand, prosperity is wealth; but it is also good health, a family that is protected and guarded daily by God's angels and it is peace, love, and joy unending. Both Kristina and Brandi have enlarged our family with 3 children each. I expect that all my children and grandchildren for generations to come will be doers of the Word of God and the words of this book.

INTRODUCTION

THE POWER OF CHOICE

God's plan for increase focuses on four things: a vision, a plan, covenant and a purpose. Many people do not make the right choices, financial or otherwise, because of three things: they do not have a vision for their life, they do not have a plan on how to get there, and they do not understand the purpose for a plan. Many people never create life choices because they haven't established a vision for their finances and established short-term and long-term goals. Proverbs 29:18 tells us people perish for lack of a vision. Most people never have a vision of becoming debt-free and accumulating wealth. It is easy to dream about "the good life," thinking of what it would be like if you were a millionaire. Anyone in a hammock with a glass of lemonade on a sunny Saturday afternoon can do that. But a dream without a measurable strategy to achieve it is nothing more than an unfulfilled vision.

Chick-Fil-A, a quality fast food industry leader, lists their statement of corporate purpose/vision as follows: "To glorify God by being a faithful steward of all that is entrusted to us and to have a positive influence on all who come in contact with Chick-Fil-A." I wrote *Debt, You're Fired; Wealth, You're Hired* to glorify God through practical, Biblical-based teaching on debt reduction, the wealth-building process, and leadership strategies. I personally created the architecture of the enclosed interactive spending plan CD which helps you defeat debt.

I want to make it as simple as possible for you and your family to develop your vision to fire debt. I want to make a positive influence on your life now, and for years to come. I pledge to help you navigate through the process from your current net worth to abundance. You *can* be debt-free and build wealth! My intent is to release a spirit of expectation in you that fuels your passion to accomplish your life *and* financial goals. My wife, Carla, and I may have been young when we set out on our journey, but we also believed that God is no respecter of persons. You may be getting a later start, but when you purpose to prosper, God will restore the years of debt that the locust has eaten (Joel 2:25). What you are getting in *Debt, You're Fired, Wealth, You're Hired* is a successful, "field-tested" strategy condensed into bite-sized steps that helps launch you into your destiny.

In *Debt, You're Fired; Wealth, You're Hired*, you learn the difference between a dream and a vision. You will see how using your power of choice unlocks the key to the process for moving from "Debt City" into becoming debt-free. You will learn how to stay focused on your plan in spite of setbacks. We outline a strategy for developing your financial vision. But we don't stop there. We teach you how to move from "Debt City" to the land of increase.

Here is some insight into my viewpoint on debt: Carla and I were married on June 19, 1971. We became engaged in 1969 on her 16th birthday, while she was a junior in high school. I was 19 and a sophomore in college. We were the typical young couple who thought they knew more than we actually did (like most teenagers!). What made us unique was the fact that as a young couple, we developed our strategy for managing money. Our vision was to acquire wealth. We developed a plan for managing our money while we were preparing for our marriage. We completed our first budget before we got married, and we made this declaration: we would never pay a penny in interest on a credit card. Thirty-five years later, Carla and I have never paid a penny in interest on a credit card and never will. We've been debt-free since 1989. We were successful for three reasons: 1) we made a choice; 2) we took a stand and 3) we had a plan.

America's view on debt has changed tremendously in the past 40 years. At the time of this writing, the typical household in America has net assets of $93,100, mostly in home equity. This family has net financial assets including retirement accounts of $23,000, down 22% from 2001. What went wrong? In the decade of the 90's as America experienced an economic boom, Americans' net financial assets declined as they spent more than they were making even as their salary appreciated. Lifestyles are adjusted easily upward in good economic times but not easily adjusted downward in tough economic times.

Although the United States may be in the midst of the longest running economic boom in its history, more than half of American households (56 percent) are behind where they should be in saving for a comfortable retirement. A related survey reported that an even larger majority of Americans (59 percent) expect that their standard of living in retirement will be lower than it is now.

That survey report was written one month after the market collapse that began in March 2000. That collapse followed a great bull market of the 90's. On March 9, 2000, the NASDAQ peaked at over 5,047. On April 11, 2006, it closed at 2,310. It still has yet to recover like the DOW and the S&P have. The NASDAQ must increase 119% just to get back where it was when this article was written. If the United States experienced the longest economic boom in history in the 1990's, why were more than 56% of Americans were behind on retirement savings then. How many more are behind today? One report noted that more than 40% of households headed by a person between the ages of 47 and 64 will not be able to replace even half of their retirement income once they stop working. Nearly 20% will have incomes below the poverty level.

In April 2006, retirement confidence has reversed although retirement savings has not increased. In other words, many Americans approach retirement only from an emotional perspective and not fact based. The Employee Benefit Research Institutes annual retirement confidence survey found that nearly 68% of workers are confident about having adequate funds for a comfortable retirement. However, 53% of people surveyed have less than $25,000 in retirement savings and an additional 12% have less than $50,000 saved for retirement. 65% of the people think they have less than $50,000 in lifetime retirement savings. This will not be enough. How much will you need? This book can begin your process to answer this question. I believe everyone should calculate what I call the *winning score*, your forecasted retirement nest egg amount that would insure a successful financial retirement.

I believe we are at a critical time in America's economic cycles. I believe we will experience a few more years of a good economy followed by a recession. I am not being prophetic with this statement. But I am rationalizing the historical trends of America's economy. Look at the past decades and you will see America has gone into a recession in each of the first years of a new decade. I encourage you to look beyond your current financial situation. This requires a financial vision statement. Both Abraham and Joseph went through famines in the book of Genesis. But because they had a vision, and never lost sight of their goals, they prospered even in the darkest times. David said in Psalm 23 that he walked through the valley of the shadow of death. You must create a winning attitude and not become afraid of your valleys. You too can walk through the debt valley. Remember, just beyond adversity is abundance.

Debt has become the friend of too many people. To defeat debt, you have to view debt as your mortal enemy. *Debt! You're Fired!* This must be your mentality. You must fire debt if you are to avoid the statistics I mentioned, but firing debt is not enough. If you fire debt -- you must *hire wealth* in its place. By hiring wealth, your job as a manager of wealth must be to make money work for you. Debt works *against* you by charging you interest. Wealth works *for* you by paying you interest. You cannot just prefer to fire debt. To change your convictions about debt, you have to move from the land of preference to conviction. Once you fire debt, you must create a "job opening" (through establishing systematic savings and investing) that allows you to hire wealth. Very few people have the capabilities to simultaneously carry debt and accumulate wealth.

A person who only prefers to do something can be negotiated out of that preference. A person with a conviction will never be moved, no matter how skillful or influential the negotiator is. Debt has become the friend of too many people. In order to defeat debt, you must view it as your mortal enemy – because it is. Are you willing to form a conviction that debt is your enemy so you can move from debt to wealth? Will you develop a financial vision and establish goals to conquer debt? Will you make a conscious decision to move from the land of preference and develop a conviction that you will be an overcomer and defeat debt in your life once and forever?

Today is a critical time in your financial life. It doesn't matter where you have been or what your current financial situation is. Your future starts NOW. You can't change the past. The present only changes when you begin a new process that in turns develops good habits. You have the ability to become a financial leader. You are a winner. You were created to have dominion. You are created to be more than a conqueror. As you begin reading *Debt, You're Fired, Wealth, You're Hired*, take a few moments to incorporate these thoughts into your belief system. Begin to believe that you CAN conquer debt. Choose to become an overcomer. As you see yourself living the life you desire, you will begin to see victory in your life. My pastor, Joel Osteen of Lakewood Church in Houston Texas, always reminds us to have a "vision of victory." I encourage you to create your vision of victory for your finances. I am honored to be the Director of the Financial Ministry at Lakewood Church. Through my ministry at Lakewood Church and Godsmoneyman.org, we have helped thousands of people create their spending plan to become debt free and begin hiring wealth.

God does not care about what you possess; He cares about what possesses you. I am not teaching a plan that delivers more things or possessions into your life. I am teaching a process of getting control over your finances and becoming a steward for God with these finances. Always remember, possessions are just material items. True wealth is from God and much broader than just material wealth. There is nothing wrong in living in a nice home or driving a fine car as long as these items don't possess you. When debt is eliminated from your life, you have more choices.

Be encouraged! Develop your vision of victory in your finances and walk through the valley of debt. God has not called you to be a statistic; He has called you to be a testimony. Get ready to begin a process that will create your financial testimony about how you defeated debt.

Greg Petsch
April, 2006

1
DEBT IS A FOUR-LETTER WORD

Train up a child in the way he should go: and when he is old, he will not depart
from it. The rich rule over the poor and the borrower is servant to the lender.
— *Proverbs 22:6-7 KJV*

When I was a young boy, my dad made it clear if we ever said a bad word, he would wash our mouths out with soap. To this day, I remember my experience with soap in my mouth. It made an impression on me and made me think before I spoke. Today, advertising agencies sell us soaps with pleasant-sounding names such as Joy or Dove. You would never connect something with a name like "Dove" as a deterrent. Unfortunately, the acceptance of four-letter words is now commonplace in our society. It's fairly easy to get a young child to change and not use bad words. But the older a child gets, the more difficult it gets. The same can be said for getting people to consider debt an exception and not a norm. God's children must learn the gift of delayed gratification in their spending in order to experience his full financial purpose for their lives.

My family lived in much simpler, slower times. I was the second of seven children and the oldest son. My dad worked for more than 30 years as an accountant for a major oil company. My mom, meanwhile, stayed home and raised the children. After the youngest child began school, Mom went back to college and obtained her nursing degree. Dad taught me how to manage and provide for the family, both then and for the future. Since he established financial boundaries; we were brought up to live within our means. Money didn't seem to be an issue with anyone; if you didn't have money you didn't buy anything.

I launched my first business at 14 years of age as a paper boy. I had to not only deliver papers each morning and evening, but I also had to sell to people who weren't taking the paper. At the end of every month, I went door-to-door collecting the money for the next month's papers. Later, my manager would come to my house to collect the money for the total papers. Any money I collected in excess of this charge was my pay for the month. I had to manage my money to the penny. My experience as a 14-yr. old small business manager helped me to understand how capitalism works at a very basic level. On one side of the equation, I learned that I had to pay for the cost of goods sold, i.e. the newspapers. On the other side, I learned to map my money to my own financial goals. I didn't realize at the time that my dad was teaching me the principle of Proverbs 22:7. I gained knowledge that I would use for bigger financial decisions throughout my entire life. Learning about money at this age was fun – because I only had the assets side of the net worth equation to deal with. I learned that my manager would not accept debt. I couldn't borrow from the papers that I would deliver. I had to pay for them in full before I delivered them. This life lesson was rooted in my financial DNA. It continues to root deeper as I teach this principle to my children; they, in turn, teach it to their own children.

In Proverbs 22:7b, we see one very good reason why we are instructed to train our children. It reads, "The rich rules over the poor, and the borrower is subject to the lender (KJV). If you are a parent, you can grasp the knowledge in *Debt, You're Fired* and make changes in your finances for yourself. Then you can teach your children how to connect to your family's vision to do the same. I believe those seeds that you planted in your kids will flourish as they apply the Biblical principles to their own lives and families. The best teaching is by example. Our education system is not teaching children how to manage money. Our government is not being a good example of how to manage money. Most publicly traded corporations are not doing a good job of showing us how to properly manage money. We cannot and should not delegate teaching our children this important responsibility. It is OUR responsibility to train our children how to manage money.

Our children watch what we do and mimic it. They will not listen to a parent's instruction to change their behavior without supporting action from that parent. If you take this knowledge and start to make simple changes, you can have an impact for generations to come. Deuteronomy 7:9 "Know therefore that the LORD your God is God; he is the faithful God, keeping his covenant of love to a thousand generations of those who love him and keep his commands." NIV

THE SPIRIT OF POVERTY – THE FATHER OF DEBT

The wealth of the rich is their fortified city, but poverty is the ruin of the poor.
— Proverbs 10:25

God is a God of abundance. The Bible says in Proverbs 3:33 that God "blesses the home of the righteous." Jesus said in John 10:10 that "The thief cometh not, but for to steal, and to kill, and to destroy: I am come that they might have life, and that they might have it more abundantly." How, then, did we get to the point where we are in lack? I believe it is because of a spirit of poverty.

The word poverty comes from a word that means "small means" or "scarceness." Poverty describes the state of being in lack. But the state of poverty does not begin with the lack. Poverty begins with the spirit of "not enough." The spirit of poverty is a liar. It tells a person that the way things are today is the way things will always be. It tells us that what we have in our hands today is the most we will ever have. In Genesis 1, you can see the seeds of the spirit of "not enough." Cain chose not to provide God with the offering He required. Surely Abel did not provide the last remaining animal available for sacrifice. God even uses people to keep us away from poverty. In Genesis 45, Joseph warned his family of their short window of opportunity to move to the land of Goshen; so that "you and your household and all that are yours may not come to poverty." (AMP)

The spirit of poverty stems from three main sources:

1. **Wrong thinking, wrong attitudes and spiritual forces.** When you get in agreement with the spirit of poverty, you allow it access into your life. People with wrong thinking often say things like, "well, maybe the Lord doesn't want me to have money." Yet, they find themselves fearful and worried about the future.

2. **Wrong believing.** Wrong believing isn't content to question whether God wants to prosper you. It causes you to flat-out believe He doesn't want to prosper you. I encourage you to do a self-check on your belief about debt and prosperity.

3. **Wrong action / not taking action.** Some people have suffered misfortune, like an accident or a layoff, which throws off their financial plan. Before they know it, there is not enough money for the month. Sometimes they resort to "robbing Peter to pay Paul" to keep a handle on things. But if they become despondent, the spirit of procrastination comes in. They never "get around to" paying the bills, or they rely on borrowing money till payday instead of planning around pay periods. Sometimes they may be under a generational financial curse that needs to be broken. Or, like the person in Psalm 1, they are "standing in the way" (associating) with people who convince them that firing debt and hiring wealth is not a priority. The fruit of this path is ruin.

Once the seed of poverty has been planted, it blossoms and grows into bitter fruit:

• **Hoarding.** Some people do not overspend. Instead, they hoard (collect and store) unnecessary quantities of things for fear of losing it all. Perhaps they were raised in financial shambles, or experienced a serious financial loss (divorce, etc.). As a result, like Scarlett O'Hara in *Gone with the Wind*, they declare to themselves, "As God is my witness; I'll never be poor again!" They carefully save anything from pieces of aluminum foil to plastic zip-seal bags. Some of them may overspend, but think they are in abundance because they hoard things they consider important, such as food or clothes. One thing is clear: Hoarding still stems from a poverty (not enough) spirit. Abundance is not the same thing as having large collections of "stuff."

• **Generational lack.** Poverty is cyclical. If adults don't learn, understand and apply sound teaching on financial abundance, they often pass the misinformation or unsound financial teaching on to their children. This creates a generation of kids who think it is normal to owe far more than they own.

• **Overspending.** Overspenders gain a sense of self-worth when they are spending money. High-end retail stores recognize this. They cater to people who overspend. They provide them with special perks, like preferred shopping times and "gifts-with-purchase," to enhance their shopping experience. In Las Vegas, the term for this type of spender is "high-roller." They are treated with extravagant hotel suites and free meals in exchange for the opportunity to be separated from their money through gambling. There are overspenders at the "normal" end of the economic spectrum too. They buy smaller luxury items, or indulge in hobbies they can't afford, to fund their drive to feel important. This also compensates for the fact that they don't have their basic necessities covered. They may still be in Debt City – but they look good.

THE SPIRIT OF DEBT

Debt, defined in simple terms, is spending tomorrow's paycheck today. Debt leads you to spend your future to impact your present. A Google search on the word "debt" produces *318 million* entries. A Google search on the word "wealth" produces *272 million* entries. One can surmise that the world is interested in these two words.

God calls debt a stranger in Deuteronomy 28. Its brother, poverty, is a peace-killer. Think of the stressful places in your life. How many of them are tied to debt and poverty? Do you stay up late at night, surrounded by "due by" envelopes,

> *Do your finances make you fearful about your future?*

wondering how you will handle them? Do you dream of sending your children to a better school? Do you and your spouse argue about unpaid bills? Would you like to be able to purchase a better car, but can't because debt has affected your credit rating? Do your finances make you fearful about your future?

There can be a lot of shame associated with debt, from the humiliation of car repossession to the catastrophe of an eviction. Some of the shame stems from feeling like a failure. Everyone else can balance their checkbook, why can't I? I did everything I knew to do, why did I get evicted? You are not alone. Countless others went through financial difficulty and were still able to leave Debt City. You will too.

One of the reasons people go into debt is because of the pressure not to delay gratification. Advertising agencies target consumers so they can condition us to "buy now, pay later." Television, radio and especially the Internet introduce us to new technological gadgets that appeal to our sense of belonging. We are enticed to buy clothing to keep up with current fashion, even though our closet is full of good clothes. We are inundated with automobile commercials and advertisements that appeal to our desires. We trade in a good older car for a new one that comes with five or six years of payments. There's nothing wrong with any of these items if you truly can afford them. I strongly recommend learning how to pay cash for the "big ticket" items – including cars. That way, there isn't a negative impact on your vision and long-term goals. If you don't learn the lesson of delayed gratification now, you will constantly be in debt. You will be trapped in the cycle of paying the interest but never receiving the interest. Implementing successfully the delayed gratification strategy will deliver you from the desire to keep up with the Jones's. If you keep trying to "keep up with the Jones's," you will never accomplish your vision and goals. You can't focus on another person and simultaneously focus on your destiny and purpose. Look at this from another angle. If your desire in life is to keep up with the Jones's, this is limited thinking because God wants to fulfill His purpose in your life; not just get you to the level of the Jones's.

DEBT IS FORFEITING YOUR FUTURE

Spend some quality time reading Deuteronomy 28. In the first 14 verses, God communicates to His children where He wants us to live. In verse 13, He tells us we should be the lender and not the borrower; the head and not the tail, above and not beneath. Note that in Deuteronomy 28:43 (KJV), God calls debt a stranger. He continues in verse 45; calling it a curse that will pursue you and overtake you until you are destroyed. (NLT) Why then, do people

> *If God calls debt a stranger, shouldn't we?*

act excited when they obtain credit approval for purchases? A (human) stranger is not allowed access to your home – but debt is welcomed.

If God calls debt a stranger, shouldn't we? I encourage you to begin NOW to open your mind and heart to receive the instructions that follow in subsequent chapters. In order to defeat an enemy, you need your own personal plan. It is one thing to read about other people's experiences. It's much better to create your own experiences. Your experiences become your testimonies.

It is estimated that only 2% of Americans live totally debt-free including their home. I encourage you to aim high in your finances. When you desire to become debt-free, you will fulfill your plan and purpose in life. First you have to fire debt, in order to move higher and create a job opening for wealth to occupy.

We have developed a financial mentality that is only concerned with what the monthly payment will be. In order to fire your debt, you need to understand what the *total cost of ownership* is. In the next chapter we will discuss many debt facts that exist in America today. When I talk about the total cost of ownership, I am referring to the cost of the product PLUS the interest over the life of the loan. When I sit down to create a spending plan for a person, the first thing we do is create a net worth statement. In the debt section of the net worth statement, I explain that the real debt we are attacking is the principle plus the interest. In many cases, the interest is as large as or larger than the amount of debt. When you go into debt, you are literally forfeiting your future!

FIRING YOUR DEBT, FUELING YOUR FUTURE

An important key to begin firing debt is to develop a "snapshot" of your current financial condition. When you analyze your total debt plus interest, then compare the interest you are scheduled to pay over the life of your loans to your lifetime savings, you will probably be shocked how much larger the interest you are paying is compared to what you have saved. We have become a nation of spenders; a saver is a rare breed today. A saver with investment knowledge is even rarer.

DECIDE TO MAKE DEBT A STRANGER

And forgive us our debts, as we forgive our debtors.
— Matthew 6:12 KJV

There are many companies that are willing to help you do something about your debt situation. Some are structured as for profit companies and others are non profit. However, in both cases, they are in business to make money. With the customized *Debt, You're Fired* spending plan CD; you learn how to understand *your own* finances. You learn how to prepare a spending plan that not only gets you out of debt, but helps you stay out. God created you to be unique for a time such as this. The spending plan is not designed to be one size fits all; instead, it puts you on a path to help you accomplish your vision and goals. You will customize the spending plan for you; therefore you begin the process of becoming the financial head of your money. Chapter 4 will provide the details for you to accomplish this.

There are two types of spenders. One spends money before they make it; the other delays spending to improve their future. Your ability to defer spending is the foundation for you to have success in debt-firing and wealth-hiring. When you learn the art of deferring gratification, you create an important character quality in your life. The skill of deferred gratification is often perfected through savings. Savings then becomes the vehicle for investments, which produces wealth. Without the ability to defer gratification, without a financial vision, without financial goals, great abundance will pass through your bank accounts and into the lenders bank account. Undirected wealth often results in great waste. If you make a conscious, continual decision to defer spending now, you will find yourself with vastly improved choices in the future.

Before you even embark on this journey you must make one decision: you must *decide to make debt a stranger*. This will take everything within you, but the results are well worth it. I have seen countless miracles happen through my God's Money Man program as people begin to live the life they never dreamed of. A Houston couple put their spending plan together and wrote me the following note:

> Greg, God has really been stirring our hearts (a fresh stirring a new revelation) regarding our finances and God's money. It is so exciting when God begins to show us our debt-free future! Thank you for all the wisdom you have poured into us. The blessings will come back to you in abundance!

Here's another testimony from one of our Financial Biblical Coaches (FBC) at Lakewood Church:

> When I entered this program my wife and I had 12 credit cards; most of them were nearing their limit. As of today, we have one credit card which we expect to pay off by the end of March. After we paid off my wife's car, we directed $2,300 to debt reduction. We have more than we ever had in savings, and have given more to God than we ever have before. Thank you for giving me the tools, scripture and software to get us where we are. To God be the glory!

RELEASING A SPIRIT OF EXPECTANCY

But remember the LORD your God, for it is he who gives you the ability to produce wealth, and so confirms his covenant, which he swore to your forefathers, as it is today.
— *Deuteronomy 8:18 NIV*

Expectancy is a catalyst for your financial vision and goals. When you *expect* to be debt free, and *expect* to successfully accumulate wealth, you accelerate your future financial success. There is not a morning that goes by when I don't think of Psalm 62:5: "My soul waits upon God for my expectation is from Him." I awake each day expecting God to move in my life, in my finances, guard my health, protect my family, open up doors of opportunity for me, give me wisdom, and grant me favor. I *expect* to have new testimonies each day. I *expect* to experience miracles in my finances. I *expect* to be prosperous. Do not allow debt to steal your opportunity to expect to fire debt, and subsequently, hire wealth.

Proverbs 22:6 in the Amplified Bible tells us to train up a child "in keeping with his individual gift or bent." In other words, no matter what our personality type, God will use the gifts He put in us *by design* to move us from debt to abundance. It isn't how much money you make that determines wealth; it is what you do with the money you make. I believe that even families who begin with modest means can move into abundance. With a plan and faith, all things are possible. I have found if you believe something can be done or if you believe something cannot be done, you are right. If you believe you can fire debt and hire wealth, you can. If you believe this only happens for the other guy, you are right. To change that thinking, you need to see yourself as the other guy. You become the other guy when you change your convictions about debt. You have to have faith that you can be diligent and overcome debt.

In the next chapter, you learn how to develop your financial vision and begin the process of firing your debt. Expect good things to happen as a result.

EXPECTATIONS

1. God calls debt a stranger – and so do I!
2. I will defer spending now to improve my future options.
3. I will make changes in my personal finances.
4. I will teach my children how to connect to our family's vision, so that they grow into debt-free, wealth-hiring adults.
5. I expect God to use the gifts He put in me to move me (my family) from debt to abundance.

2

DROWNING IN
DEBT CITY

*The wicked borrow and pay not again [for they may be unable], but the
[uncompromisingly] righteous deal kindly and give [for they are able].*
— Psalm 37:21 AMP

People were dancing and having a good time on the Titanic even as the ship was sinking.
America's financial ship is sinking due to debt. This chapter gives you information that
mainstream media doesn't provide. It is also intended to get your attention. I encourage
you to use the information you gain from this chapter to get on one of the life boats now
and begin rowing to shore. I am not giving you this data to depress you or to lead you
down a "gloom and doom" path. I am challenging you to decide that today can be the day
of new beginnings in your finances. You can overcome debt and live a financially-stress-
free, prosperous life. Set your vision to become one of the 2% of Americans who are
totally debt free, including their home.

I like working with numbers. Another aspect of my financial DNA is that I can never
remember a day that I was comfortable with any amount of debt. I believe that as soon
as you get comfortable with debt, debt begins the reverse compounding effect of taking
interest from you without you realizing it. Very few people ever understand this. Without

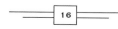

a vision, people remain short-term thinkers; they don't get past the immediate gratification of an instant 10% savings that might be offered at a store during the purchase process. They never think long-term beyond how much that purchase will cost with interest.

In 1967, when I was a junior in high school, I got a job working for a local clothing department store. My dad arranged for me to get a store credit card. I was so excited when I received this small plastic card with my name on it! Fortunately, it only had a $35 maximum balance I could charge. The next time I went into the store; I charged $35 on the card. A few weeks later I received the bill. When my dad explained the repayment process to me, I realized that I would have to pay interest on this purchase if I didn't pay it off in full. Up to this point, I had been working almost three years and only receiving interest from my savings. I made a decision to pay the credit card balance in full. I learned an important lesson: I would pay far more for a product if I charged it and did not pay it off in full each month. That was the only charge I ever made on that credit card. I carried it around with me for quite a while but was never tempted to use it again, because dad taught me about reverse compounding.

> *Decide today will be the day of new beginnings!*

MINIMUM PAYMENT = MAXIMUM INTEREST

Advertising agencies spend billions of dollars to make people think they are special if they go into debt. That's why credit card companies offer a slice of "pre-approved" plastic with several thousands of dollars of debt opportunity attached to it. People think they are even more special if they receive the gold or platinum card. They get captured by the opportunity, sign up for their credit card and, in some stores, receive an immediate 10% discount. Retailers don't mind this 10% discount; they know they will reap a larger return on the interest you will pay them. Remember, the credit card company's vision is to keep you in bondage, so they can make money from you. They have no interest in showing you how to get out of credit card debt. In fact, their bills offer you another benefit that benefits them; the bill is for the minimum amount. If you pay only the minimum you might think; this is good because I can afford this minimum monthly payment. The credit card company knows it is good – for them. This way, they get the maximum interest payment from you!

FOLLOW THE MONEY

Debt is a four letter word. You have to have a conviction with this statement if you are going to fire debt. America is a blessed country. We are a little over 230 years old with a population approximately 300 million people, yet the world's largest economy as measured by Gross Domestic Product, GDP. America now exceeds $12.4 trillion dollars in GDP. How blessed are we? The world's total GDP is estimated to be $59.38 trillion. Therefore, America represents over 20% of the total GDP in the world. Measuring our population, we comprise about 5% of the world people. Capture this comparison. At 230 years old, America is like a teenager compared to the rest of the world in Europe, the Middle East and Africa.

When we analyze our country's debt, we learn that the larger our economy the more tax revenue that comes in. However, our spending outpaces our income. We have had both Republicans and Democrats in control of the White House and Congress during the past few decades, yet our nation's debt increases, no matter which party is in charge. For the 2007 budget, President Bush submitted a spending plan for $2.77 trillion and income of $2.41 trillion; a planned shortage of $354 billion in addition to the $423 billion shortage in 2006.

How much debt is there? Let's begin by dissecting the debt of our Federal Government. In January 2006, America broke through the $8 trillion debt ceiling on April 12, 2006; it has now accumulated $8.4 trillion in debt. In 2005, our federal debt increased by over $400 billion or over $100,000 for every baby born in 2005. Now, debt has accelerated to $400 billion increase in less than 4 months. If every citizen of America were to equally pay the debt off, each man, woman and child would pay $26,750. This is a large number but realize it is growing every day as well because of the interest on this debt. America has never defaulted on its financial obligations because it has the ability to continue to print money to pay for the debts. The effects of running our nation's money printing presses results in the value of our money decreasing. The following table from the Bureau of Public Debt shows the tremendous growth of our nation's debt:

Prior Fiscal Years	Debt
09/30/2005	$7,932,709,661,723.50
09/30/2003	$6,783,231,062,743.62
09/30/2002	$6,228,235,965,597.16
09/28/2001	$5,807,463,412,200.06
09/29/2000	$5,674,178,209,886.86
09/30/1999	$5,656,270,901,615.43
09/30/1998	$5,526,193,008,897.62
09/30/1997	$5,413,146,011,397.34
09/30/1996	$5,224,810,939,135.73
09/29/1995	$4,973,982,900,709.39
09/30/1994	$4,692,749,910,013.32
09/30/1993	$4,411,488,883,139.38
09/30/1992	$4,064,620,655,521.66
09/30/1991	$3,665,303,351,697.03
09/28/1990	$3,233,313,451,777.25
09/29/1989	$2,857,430,960,187.32
09/30/1988	$2,602,337,712,041.16
09/30/1987	$2,350,276,890,953.00

There's a song that contains a line, "One man's ceiling is another's man's floor." President Bush has raised the national debt ceiling four times since 2001. In 2000, the approved national debt ceiling was *$5.75 trillion*. There's a logical conclusion here: there is no difference in the way we financially manage our country as to the way the average American manages their finances. It is out of control! Someday, America will have to face the music and realize the floor has to become the ceiling. A question for parents; do you realize your children will have to pay for this debt through increases in personal tax rates?

The financial sector debt in America has grown to almost $12.5 trillion. This is primarily attributed to the addition of Fannie Mae and Freddie Mac, companies providing government backed mortgages. Since 1957, this section of debt has increased 23 times faster than the economy has grown including inflation. The business sector debt in America has grown to $8.3 trillion. Ford is America's largest business debtor and General Motors is number three. Indications of the effects of unaddressed debt can be seen in 2006 announcements by both of these companies with 25,000 to 30,000 layoffs each and manufacturing plant closures. If this can happen to foundation companies that were key contributors to America's rise

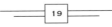

as an economic powerhouse, what is stopping this from occurring in your finances or the company you work for? These large announced layoffs of employees are just the tip of the iceberg. Below the water is a supply base feeling the tsunami of the poor financial management of Ford and General Motors. This affects thousands of additional employees of companies that supply products and services to these two large corporations. Debt has raised its ugly head at Ford; a company that recently celebrated its 100th birthday. Debt is not a respecter of the aged. Debt will come against both young and old. Is your household protected against a loss of a paycheck for any length of time? If not, I encourage you to begin creating your vision and continue reading this book.

The consumer debt in America has also grown tremendously. Twenty years ago, consumer debt in America was approximately $15,000 per person. Today, it has grown to approximately $36,750 per person. Therefore, a family of four carries debt averaging approximately $147,000. The main components of consumer debt in America are mortgages and credit cards. It is estimated that consumer debt is approximately $11.5 trillion. Mortgages represent approximately $7.5 trillion and credit cards more than $2 trillion. The consumer drives our economy. With America's economy at more than $12.4 trillion, two-thirds of this GDP is created by the consumer. Almost half of credit card borrowers are only paying the minimums each month. Home equity is at an all time low as Americans have borrowed from their equity for various reasons and automobiles can now be financed for six years. These are all indications of a financially-strapped nation.

A CHOICE WITH CONVICTION

When you add all the debt of the above sectors and add the state and local government debt, it totals more than *$44 trillion*. As a percentage of our GDP it is 355%. Never has the debt in America as a percentage of our GDP been this high; not even during the Great Depression of 1929 through 1939. There is no end in sight for this increase of the debt levels in America. It is now decision time for you. Only you can make this decision and make it with conviction. Are you willing to begin to control your financial future? It is a choice you have.

> *There will come a day, very soon, when all of us will have to pay up.*

But a choice without action is a dream. Your choice to fire debt will allow you to control your financial destiny. Failing to make this choice with conviction will result in your destiny being controlled by the lender. Remember, Deuteronomy 28:13 God tells us He wants you to be the lender and not the borrower. He wants you to be the head and not the tail, He wants you to be above and not beneath. This is His desire for you. Do you possess the same desire? God tells us He has given us the ability to produce wealth that He may establish His covenant in us. He also tells us in Psalm 35:27 that He takes pleasure in your prosperity.

President George H.W. Bush coined the phrase "voodoo economics." It basically means we can have our money and spend it too. No one at the upper levels of our government is taking a stand and saying "enough is enough." We are experiencing the effects of voodoo economics. It has manifested in our governments, in our business, and in the households of almost all of our citizens. This isn't magic I am talking about. All of this debt isn't created by smoke and mirrors. Almost all individuals think they can continue with their own voodoo economics and never have to pay the piper. That is false security. There will come a day, very soon, when all of us – the government, the businesses and the consumers – will have to pay up. Beginning today, start to separate your financial life from the financial crisis that results from poor stewardship or fiscal irresponsibility.

DEVELOPING A DEBT-FREE MINDSET

Thirty-three percent of U.S. born-again Christians say it is impossible for them to get ahead in life because of the financial debt they have incurred. It is time to separate your own money management process from the world's money management process. The world's system is to get you into debt and keep you there. God's financial system is to get you through the debt-firing process and on the way to prospering. Are you ready to make this choice? Are you ready to disembark the world's financial Titanic and embark on a new journey? There is

> *It's what you do with what you earn that determines your success.*

never a better time to begin than today. I encourage you to not delay. Some people think, "If I only made more money I could fire debt." In reality, it's what you do with what you earn that determines success.

Now is the time to think, yes, I can fire debt. Tell yourself that these statistics are not for you. I will separate my financial life from the average American. It will take a plan to accomplish this. It begins with your thought. Proverbs 23:7 tells us that you are what you think in your heart. Begin believing, no matter what your situation is right now, that you can fire debt and hire wealth. See yourself succeeding. You have to begin thinking like a debt-free person thinks.

MENTALITY OF A DEBT-FIRER

1. Debt-firers believe that debt steals your purpose and destiny.
2. Debt-firers avoid people who tell them becoming debt-free isn't possible.
3. Debt-firers make choices on purchases based upon the money they have, not money from a creditor.
4. Debt-firers have a strategy for increase. This validates their goals as they distribute the increase.
5. Debt-firers look where they are going – not where they have been.
6. Debt-firers manage their money – and don't ever let their money manage them.
7. Debt-firers believe that financial freedom comes when debt is gone.
8. Debt-firers believe their money is their *employee*. They make sure every employee knows the job expected from them.

Every day is a learning opportunity. We are surrounded by knowledge, information and statistics. The Bible (KJV) mentions money 140 times. Take time each day to read God's Word. Read it and also financial periodicals like Money Magazine or Kiplinger's to learn something new about money and how it works. Ignorance is no excuse when you retire. If you retire without enough money, it will not be because you did not make enough money. It will be because you didn't have a financial vision and stay focused on your goals. Until you are ready to fire your debt, you will never be in a position to hire wealth. *Debt is standing between you and your financial vision.*

Ye have compassed this mountain long enough: turn you northward.
— Deuteronomy 2:3 KJV

MOVING OUT OF DEBT CITY

You will not move forward until you refuse to live in Debt City. When you live in Debt City, you lose accountability. As soon as you lose accountability, you are destined to lose responsibility. You lose accountability when you look at your money in terms of monthly payments instead of the cost of the total cost of the purchase plus interest. You have become the borrower and work for the lender. You lose responsibility because the lender tells you where and when you must pay your money. You lose stability because you spend in excess of your income. As you lose responsibility and accountability, you will lose stability. Moving out of Debt City can be scary; especially if you've lived there a long time. I told you one reason for poverty is fear and unbelief. You think, "I can't do this, I can't become debt-free." 'I can't' is the brother of 'I don't want to.' You can do this. Beginning today, you can prepare a plan and fire debt. Followers populate Debt City, but overcomers are able to leave Debt City and become leaders. The good news is, the Bible says we are overcomers! The statistics in this chapter are not encouraging. If this chapter was written last year, the amount of debt would be less but still staggering. If it was written a year from now, it will be much larger than what I am reporting today. Are you going to ride the storm out, or are you going to get out of Debt City? It is worth the move. *You can do this.* Remember, followers populate Debt City; but overcomers are able to leave Debt City and become leaders. Leaders become mentors.

In the next chapter, you will learn how to develop your financial vision, how to give yourself permission to prosper, and create an atmosphere of order that empowers you to succeed. Get ready to move out of Debt City!

EXPECTATIONS

1. I will stop paying the minimum amount on my credit cards.
2. I will develop a debt-free mindset starting today.
3. I will change my money management process from the world's process.
4. I will develop an accountability system that prepares me to move out of Debt City.
5. I will not let fear and unbelief keep me bound in Debt City.
6. I will begin the process of living within my income.

3

DEVELOPING YOUR FINANCIAL VISION

Where there is no vision, the people perish: but he that keepeth the law,
happy is he.
— Proverbs 29:18 KJV

As I mentioned before, I began my business career on my first day in the ninth grade. I delivered newspapers for the *Beaumont Enterprise* and *Journal* in Beaumont Texas. Mr. Green, my boss, would knock on my bedroom window at four a.m. to wake me up for my delivery run. I also delivered afternoon papers six days a week after school. I continued this routine seven days a week, 365 days a year. I earned an average of $85 a month, and saved an average of $68 a month. I had a vision for the use of my earnings. My dad told me I couldn't buy a car until I graduated from high school. So, I set my sights on earning enough money to buy the car of my choice when I graduated. I worked four different jobs throughout high school, but my vision didn't change. I opened a savings account and made a deposit from every paycheck. Then, my dad taught me the miracle of saving and compounding interest. I began placing my earnings into an interest-bearing savings account. By the beginning of my senior year, Dad introduced me to the stock market. I bought my first stock at age 17. I tracked my stock's profit every day in the newspaper. In one month, January 1968, I made more than $2,000 in the stock market – more money than the cumulative interest on my savings account from the previous three years. This immediately gave me the power to buy a shiny new 1968 Chevrolet Camaro, with cash,

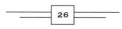

when I graduated. When you are burdened with debt, you limit your choices. The creditors dictate your lifestyle. As you fire debt and hire wealth, you begin to have choices in your money decisions.

> *A farmer sowed his field and went away, and as the days went by, the seeds grew and grew without his help. For the soil made the seeds grow. First a leaf-blade pushed through, and later the wheat-heads formed and finally the grain ripened, and then the farmer came at once with his sickle and harvested it.*
> *— Mark 4:26-29*

This is what I experienced when I invested in the stock market. As you gradually plant (seed investment) in the ground, at the appointed time it will break forth and bring in a tremendous harvest. (Galatians 6:9).

VISIONS VS. DAYDREAMS

I mentioned Chick-Fil-A's statement of corporate purpose (vision) in my introduction. Let me repeat it to you again:

"To glorify God by being a faithful steward of all that is entrusted to us and to have a positive influence on all who come in contact with Chick-Fil-A."

I have heard from several sources that Chick-Fil-A makes more money in six days than their competitors do in seven. There are fast food restaurants – and then there is Chick-Fil-A. What makes this fast food restaurant different? They use the same grease, have similar stainless steel equipment, have a drive through window, clean restrooms, etc. The difference begins with their *vision*. Several years ago I worked with a company to help develop their business plan. I read Chick-Fil-A's vision to my colleagues. The next week, when I returned for our strategy meeting, one of the executives disclosed that he tested this Chick-Fil-A vision. He went to one of the restaurants and asked each of the employees if they knew the vision statement. To his surprise, all of them knew it. A vision remains a daydream unless you make it a passion. This is the genesis of the difference in the profitability of Chick-Fil-A. All the employees buy into the vision statement. The company incorporates their vision into a training program. They emphasize customer satisfaction into every word and action. Employees always are neatly dressed. They always conclude the conversation with "My pleasure" instead of "No problem." Most importantly, they work to make each customer feel as if he or she is the most important person who ever walked into their restaurant. When your vision becomes more than a daydream, and you add processes and standards that reinforce the training, you will always experience positive results. Chick-Fil-A has set high standards for customer satisfaction and is rewarded by a loyal customer base. Your financial vision and supporting goals begin the process of setting your standards. They are also a model of a company that puts God first. Success follows them because they exist to glorify God.

PERMISSION TO PROSPER

Many people say they want more out of life. What does "more" look like to you? Is more purchasing a car without financing it? Is more moving to a safer neighborhood? Is more being able to fund your church/ministry's visions or other important causes? What would you do with more? What does more look like? Close your eyes and open your mind. Does more look like being able to send your children to college and graduate school if they'd like, without taking out a student loan?

I believe that people have difficulty answering the question, "what does 'more' look like?" for four main reasons: 1) they do not have a personal vision of what their prosperous life looks like; 2) they do not have a plan to get there; 3) they have experienced so many setbacks that they have given up. However there is another important reason, one that often derails the most well-thought out vision or plan. Some people have simply not given themselves permission to prosper. They may have or have had vision and dreams for their lives, but secretly don't believe it could happen for them. They have been disappointed so long and so often that they think a better life is what happens to "the other guy." We'll talk more about balanced teaching on prosperity in Chapter 5, but I'll say here that God *absolutely wants us to prosper*. Ephesians says God is able to do "exceedingly, abundantly above all we can ask or think." The Amplified Bible expands on this. It says "infinitely beyond our highest prayers, desires, thoughts, hopes or dreams." Here's the kicker: the last part of the verse reads "according to the power that works *in you*." God has already given you the power you need to walk out of Debt City and into financial freedom. Not everyone will be millionaires, but everyone has the potential to become debt-free.

THE FLIP SIDE OF PROSPERITY

Let's look at the flip side of prospering. Yes, there are negatives. How are you going to respond when friends who don't support your vision and maybe complain that you don't have time for them anymore? Can you manage not to feel guilty when God blesses you in your quest? Financial prosperity gives you options. Are you ready to grow accustomed to having options? How will you feel not having to live under the pressure of pressing bills? These are not rhetorical questions. Some people are so accustomed to living with the drama of being in debt that the absence of pressure seems abnormal. God is ready to help you make choices. But you have to be willing to release pressure and receive peace. Having debt is like living under the authority of a dictator. History records that once a country is delivered from the atrocities of dictatorship, society runs amuck for about a generation. Your vision and goals will keep you from running amuck when you cross the border of Debt City and move into your Canaan.

ORDER PRECEDES INCREASE

Let all things be done decently and in order.
— 1 Corinthians 14:40 KJV

Order is defined as "a condition in which each thing is properly disposed with reference to other things and to its purpose; a methodical or harmonious arrangement." In the previous section, we talked about giving yourself permission to prosper. A big part of giving permission to prosper involves creating an atmosphere of order in your life. I recommend that you make time and space to manage your money. Dedicate a regularly-scheduled time and place to review and attend to your finances. If possible, use that place ONLY for money management. Make sure your family and friends understand your money management time is "DND" (do not disturb) time. Invest in

> *Make time and space to manage your money.*

inexpensive accordion file folders, plain white envelopes, calculator and pen and paper. If the area you select is cluttered, take time to clear it out before you begin. Make your debt-firing area a pleasant place to work; a place you want to spend time. The point is to associate your workspace with a pleasant activity. You can be in control, since you know where everything is and the purpose for their presence.

Get your house in order. Has God ever spoken these words to you? Isaiah spoke these words to King Hezekiah in Isaiah 38:1: "In those days Hezekiah became ill and was at the point of death. The prophet Isaiah son of Amoz went to him and said, "This is what the LORD says: Put your house in order, because you are going to die; you will not recover." NIV

Isaiah told King Hezekiah to get his house in order because he was going to die. Immediately upon receiving this news, Hezekiah prayed to God. God gave him 15 years more time on earth. He put his house in order and his life on earth

> *Make your debt-firing area a pleasant place to work.*

was increased 15 years. King Hezekiah is one of the nine kings out of the 42 mentioned in 1 Kings and 2 Kings that God said "did good in the eyes of God." Begin today to put order in all areas of your life. You will be glad you did.

I have implemented spending plans for approximately two thousand people in the last few years with the Financial Biblical Coaches, (FBC's). Order is a common missing ingredient in finances. During my professional career, I could walk into someone's office and tell whether they had order in their life. If they had a messy desk, an office with poorly organized book shelves, and paper on the floor, blinds that were crooked, in most cases, these are indicators of lack of order in their lives. If they didn't have visible order in their office, they probably didn't have order in their finances. I can say the same experience exists in the home. If I go to someone's home to create a spending plan and I see the yard hasn't been taken care of; the flower beds are a foot high with weeds and the trimming hasn't occurred in months, probabilities are that when I enter the home, the inside will also be in disarray. I can't recall doing a spending plan at a disorderly home where there was financial order. Order is an easy thing to begin, but a difficult thing to change and maintain.

YOU ARE THE PERSON FOR THE JOB

It's time for us to put our financial house in order. It is time to rebuild the walls around our finances. It is not impossible. Nehemiah took a task that looked impossible and went to work to rebuild the walls around the city of Jerusalem. Nehemiah was not qualified by human standards to do this job. He was not an architect, he was not a bricklayer, and he was not a builder. He was, however, a man with a purpose, a man called to go and restore the order around God's city.

Nehemiah could have made excuses. He could have said "I have a job to do; I am the King's cupbearer." He could have protested, "I am not qualified." He could have made the excuse that he was too busy. He could have made the same excuses that people did for the previous 100 years while the walls around God's city were torn down. Are you making excuses for not rebuilding the walls around your finances? A city without walls is defenseless. A city without walls is a city without order. People can come and go; there is no control point for entry and exit. Is this the case for your finances? Do you have order in your financial home? Do you have a control point for entry and exit of spending to a plan? You are called to restore order in your finances. You are the person for the job! You have the authority for your Homeland Security.

> *You are called to restore order in your finances!*

God wants us to be a good steward. Jesus said in Luke 6:23: "How can you be trusted with the true riches if you can't manage the riches you have today?" He goes on to say in verse 24 that you cannot serve God and mammon. Mammon is the system invented by the Syrians of lending money and charging interest. (The word literally means "riches.") Jesus is telling us to get our house in order. Get away, far away, from this mammon system. This system will lead you into financial chaos. It is a system that has the credit company's best interest in mind, not yours. It is a system designed to get you into debt and keep you there. It is a system of bondage. It is a system that will keep you out of order with your money.

Order precedes increase! I encourage you to get your house in order. Rebuild the walls around your home. God provides a hedge of protection, but few seek it. We need to pray for God's protection and order over our home, our finances, NOW, before problems occur. Take control of your finances. Begin by following the six steps to get out of debt plan in Chapter 4. This gives you a process for order in your income and spending.

Another definition for order is "an authoritative direction or instruction." You must command your finances to come into order. What you say determines how high you fly. Your attitude does determine your altitude. Everything must be done in balance. Make time for God, make time for your family, and then make time for order in your finances.

MAPPING YOUR MONEY TO YOUR VISION

The reason it was so easy for me as a teenager to save for my car is because I had mapped my money (working for the Beaumont Enterprise newspaper) to my vision (a new car after graduation). I made purchasing a car at graduation my main priority. This helped keep me from activities that distracted me from my goal. My money never had an opportunity to burn a hole in my pocket, so to speak. Haggai 1:6 TLB says your income disappears as though you were putting it into pockets filled with holes. To avoid this occurrence, you can map your money to your vision too. Let's start with where your priorities have been to date, starting with your checkbook. I can immediately tell where your priorities lie by looking at your checkbook register. Here's an experiment to try. Pick up a small, inexpensive notepad. Write down every purchase or expense you make for the next thirty days. You will be amazed how small purchases add up. This chart can be helpful in Chapter 4 as you use the enclosed spending plan CD to create your plan.

SHORT-TERM THINKING, LONG-TERM GOALS

A human's vision is measured in close-up vision and distance vision. Financial vision is comprised of short-term *and* long-term goals. Many people never create choices in their life, because they haven't established a vision for their finances broken down into short- term and long-term goals. Short-term thinking alone results in short-term actions with no lasting positive result. However, long-term thinking should contain a series of short-term steps designed to propel you into the future. A long-term thinker's natural process means staying focused on the short-term; they know the vision is for the appointed time in their future. You must remain focused. Someone once said if you chase two rabbits, both will escape. The clearest way to move out of Debt City is to first focus on what is in front of you.

> *If you chase two rabbits, both of them will escape.*

Goals will always keep you focused on your vision. This vision could be represented as the center of a target. Accomplishing your vision is like throwing a dart and hitting the bullseye. Most people today don't have a target and obviously, without a target they never are throwing their darts in the same direction each time. A vision is synonymous with a dream of a better future. Sadly, we have been turned into daydreamers instead of visionaries. Proverbs 29:18 tells us people perish for lack of a vision. A vision is a "should be," not a "could be." In other words, a vision should align to a strong sense of belonging and belief. It must reflect on your past victories and build upon your future potential.

Moving out of "Debt City" is no different than moving into a new home. Stuff needs to be thrown out; a "moving vehicle" needs to be prepared. Your "moving vehicle" is this book and the *Debt, You're Fired* spending plan CD.

DON'T STORE YOUR STUFF

Whole industries are dedicated to the storing of stuff. From Tupperware, to the Container Stores, to the large increase in storage buildings, people store their "stuff" for its protection, its preservation and its presentation. But to get a fresh start in a new home, you've got to leave some stuff behind. That's what garage sales are for. Stuff once considered priceless is now too cumbersome or outdated to keep. In order to live successfully in your future, you have to be willing to leave the Debt City mentality behind. Philippians 3:13 put it this way: "Brethren, I count not myself to have apprehended: but this one thing I do, forgetting those things which are behind…"

As you prepare to move out of Debt City, remember to leave your past behind you. Have you packed your suitcases with bitterness, fear, discord, shame? If so, leave that suitcase right where it is and never pick it up again. When establishing your vision, you should not refer back to past failures. Forgive yourself and move on. Today is a new day. Use past experiences as road material for paving your future. We have all made mistakes. Successful people use these experiences to overcome and learn, thus enabling them to move higher the next attempt. You can't change the past. But you can change your present and you can change your future.

DON'T DESPISE SMALL BEGINNINGS

As you walk though the debt-firing process, you will first see small changes followed by dramatic ones. Do not despise the day of small beginnings. Imagine for a moment what it will feel like the first morning you wake up and are totally debt free. One day you will be living a life where the bed you slept in is paid for, when the home you are in is paid for, when the car in your garage is paid for, when you owe nothing on any credit cards, when the student loan is paid off; this will help you create your vision for your finances as you begin to see the day of financial deliverance.

GET READY TO WIN!

The information I collect through the spending plan creation sessions validates many of the facts I've stated in this book. Most leave their first debt-firing sessions with hope that hasn't existed in their lives in years. They can see a customized plan for their finances in great detail. It shows them exactly when they will pay off each debt, and how they can apply the money on the now paid-off debt to the amount they pay on their next debt. An accelerated result occurs. The longest time to pay off a debt is the first debt; every debt after that is paid off much more quickly. Why? Because of the snowball effect of using debt money to stay focused on the goal of firing debt. You create your snowball by applying the money from the paid off debt to the second debt and continue this process with each *debt that is paid off.* You will have the victory when every debt is paid in full. Focusing on the snowball effect allows you to keep the money working towards debt elimination and not towards some other expense or new debt. Hope precedes faith. Hope means a favorable, confident expectation of good. Expectations begin with your thoughts. Your thoughts are powerful because they precede your words.

In the next two chapters, we help you prepare answers to the following questions:

1. Do you have a financial vision?
2. Do you have a spending plan?
3. Do you have an emergency fund?
4. Are you tithing and giving offerings?
5. Are you saving for retirement from every paycheck?
6. Are you managing your 401K investments to ensure you have five-star mutual funds?
7. Do you know what your "winning score" is for a comfortable retirement?

You will need the following:

- Your home computer with Windows 2000 or Windows XP
- A note pad and pen
- All your bills and paycheck stubs
- Your *Debt, You're Fired* spending plan CD

Pack your bags and get ready to move!

EXPECTATIONS

1. I will develop a vision of what "more" looks like in my life.

2. I will feel gratitude, not guilt, when God's abundance comes in my life.

3. I will begin to put order in my surroundings to prepare for my increase.

4. I will develop an accountability system that prepares me to move out of Debt City.

5. I will not let fear and unbelief keep me bound in Debt City.

6. I will continue to give as my harvest begins, so my harvest will come back to me multiplied.

4

SIX STEPS TO GET OUT OF DEBT

No weapon that is formed against thee shall prosper; and every tongue that shall rise against thee in judgment thou shalt condemn. This is the heritage of the servants of the LORD, and their righteousness is of me, saith the LORD.
— Isaiah 54:17 KJV

At one time in your life, you probably made a New Year's resolution to become debt-free or to better manage your money. You also probably started a budget for a few months. However, most people who begin to create a systematic process to manage money better stop for various reasons. Perhaps an unforeseen expense came up which caused you to borrow. This expense caused your plan to derail. Maybe your plan was based on overtime pay that covered all your expenses. Suddenly, your employer eliminated overtime for awhile. Now, you are short in income each paycheck. Maybe your plan was based upon a two-income plan where both spouses worked and one spouse

> *God didn't say we would never be attacked.*

lost their job. There are many life experiences that might have discouraged you. I am here to encourage you. If you follow these six steps, know that if you face an obstacle, you are going *through* it and you will achieve victory in your finances. God didn't say we wouldn't be attacked. He *did* say that none of the weapons formed against us would defeat us.

I receive encouraging testimonies from people who write after successfully implementing the six steps to get out of debt. Here are two of them. "R.T" wrote:

> The God's Money Man team helped me to create a budget/spending plan and list my financial goals. One of my goals was to own a house by the end of 1st quarter 2005. I did not make the deadline; however, I just closed on my first home yesterday! I also purchased three other rental properties, moving me closer to my goal of having other sources of income. All have been leased out prior to closing. These transactions bring me closer to my goal of financial freedom and "retirement." God has been good and I am very thankful for all of His blessings. I also thank you and Lakewood Church for providing your services through the Financial Ministry. If I hadn't written down my goals before the New Year, it would take a long time to act upon them.

Chris wrote:

> My wife and I met with you several years ago. We are in our dream house and eliminated all other debt. We owe roughly $92,892 on our home at (5.375%/ 30 years). I've figured by making an extra $500 per month payment to principal, we can pay off our home in about nine years and save almost $200K! God has really blessed us.

These two testimonies are not identical but are similar. A spending plan is not a one size fits all; however, the processes are similar no matter where you are in life. R.T had a vision of owning real estate to fund his retirement years; his family implemented a plan to accomplish this. Chris and his wife had a plan to eliminate all debts, and then use the money they paid on previous monthly bills to add to their home's monthly principal payoff. This money saved them almost $200,000 in interest.

WRITE YOUR VISION

Have you written your financial vision out yet? If not, this is the time to do it in step 1 of these six steps to get out of debt. I want you to declare these words today: I am declaring war on debt. I will fire debt. I am coming out of financial bondage and moving into financial freedom. Romans 4:17 tells us to call those things that aren't as though they were. I think it is telling us to call the things that occupy us in the world's system as God intended them

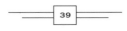

to exist in our lives. In other words, if you are in debt and your goal is to be debt-free, you need to begin to call yourself debt-free. However, you need a plan to do this.

Faith without works is dead.
— James 2:20 KJV

The opposite of faith is unbelief. Check your heart at this time to see if you have any unbelief that you can fire debt. If it exists, close this book and begin to pray and ask for God's strength to overcome this unbelief and replace it with faith. Mix your faith now with the works of implementing these six steps to get out of debt. Remember, you have to be successful in these six steps in order to fire debt. We will begin discussing hiring wealth in Chapter 5.

STEWARDSHIP, NOT OWNERSHIP

Debt is a dream slayer – but God is a dream restorer. Debt may have stolen others' dreams but you are a conqueror, an overcomer through Christ. The spending plan begins with a clear understanding of your role in accumulating wealth. You must have the correct motive. The idea in this book is not to teach you to how to become wealthy through firing debt. It is intended to teach you how to become wise stewards of God's money. Here are two definitions to help you understand stewardship: 1) taking care of someone else's possessions as if they were your own; and 2), fulfilling someone else's agenda with someone else's money. Your motive should be that you are going to use your abilities to produce wealth. Your vision should validate your purpose God has called you to fulfill here on earth. All your wealth will stay here on earth when you go to Heaven. It all belongs to Him; he has given all of us the title of steward. In other words, we are taking care of God's resources. As we do a good job, we move from being a one-talent financial person to a two-talent person striving to become a five-talent financial person according to Matthew 25. The Bible tells us all the gold and silver belongs to God. He owns the cattle on a thousand hills and spoke everything into existence. It all belongs to Him. He is looking for us to assume our position of being His stewards.

Becoming debt-free is a process. It has taken you years to accumulate the amount of debt you have. All of us would like to eliminate debt today if at all possible. This is possible though a miracle from God. Your faith should be so big that you expect God's miracles in your life. My role in this book is to give you practical plans and steps to walk out of your financial wilderness as fast as possible. If you desired to lose weight, you begin an exercise program and change your eating habits. The same idea exists today for you to fire debt. You need to begin to exercise your faith through the spending plan and spend your money in alignment to the plan you create. Since becoming debt-free is a process, you must be committed to fire debt once and only once. You must be passionate that once you come out of debt, you will never go back into debt.

YOUR SPENDING PLAN

Debt, You're Fired Windows-based spending plan CD

You received a *Debt, You're Fired* Windows-based spending plan CD with your copy of this book. Your spending plan is a software program that shows you how to accomplish your vision and goals. This chapter explains how to install and use it. Don't worry about computing the numbers. All the math formulas are in the program. All you need to do is input your numbers. The software automatically calculates for you. Once installed on your computer, review the "Help" section for a detailed instruction. Depending on the month you begin, it creates a 61 month (minimum) – 72 month (maximum) plan. I have found that almost 90% of the plans can pay off all debts within this time frame, with the exception of the mortgage. In more than 80% of the plans I develop with people, the problem is not an income shortage but a money management issue. The spending plan teaches you how to align your money to your vision and goals, and manage it every month to the penny.

I have included additional teachings on the Bible and money in the software program. Review the "Support" tab at the top of the home page for self-study. Also included in the software, under "Tools" are a mortgage calculator and a notes section for you to write to yourself what you will accomplish based upon the spending plan you create.

STEP 1 – KNOW THE FACTS (AND PREPARE)

Living Expenses +
Debt Expenses =
Your Financial Data or total expenses

Before a country goes to war, its leaders develop a war plan. All I need to say is the phrase "9-11" and you instantly know what that means. America was attacked on September 11, 2001. However, our country didn't wage war on September 12th. Our leaders formulated a plan, gave details to those in authority and began a plan to logistically move soldiers and weapons to strategic locations in Afghanistan. On October 7, 2001, America began bombing Afghanistan. American leaders did not react out of emotions; they developed a plan by first knowing the facts. In order for them to respond so effectively in less than a month, they were prepared.

You cannot go to your financial war without knowing the facts. You need a process to begin to assimilate the data. This data consists of a complete listing of all your living expenses and your debt expenses. Your debt expenses must include your current balance owed, your interest rate and your monthly payment.

"FAITH" YOUR FEARS AWAY

God has not given us the spirit of fear, but a spirit of power and love and a sound mind.
— 1st Timothy 1:7

Fear is a powerful force. It is a force that opposes faith. One Sunday after church, a gentleman approached me and asked for help in developing a spending plan. I obliged, saying the first thing I needed was for him to gather all his financial facts. "I can't do this," he replied. "I'm afraid to know how much debt I have." I told the man, "I can't help you if we don't have a place to begin." Without the knowledge of these facts, you will never fire debt. I have coached many families that are afraid just like this man was. Be comforted because fear is not from God. In Luke 12:32, God tells us to fear not little flock because it is your Father's good pleasure to give you the Kingdom. If you are fearful about your debt, begin taking authority over this fear. Eventually, this gentleman gathered his facts and we developed a plan. Today, he has conquered all debts except his mortgage.

GATHER ALL YOUR BILLS

When you have all your debts in one place add the totals. Most people don't know the total amount of their bills. As we proceed to step two, you will see this list of your debts is not the whole battle we are fighting. We will extend the data from step 1 and create a plan to defeat the debt plus the interest. While the sum of your debts you are now looking at may seem large, wait until you see how much interest you will pay on this debt and how many months it will take you to pay it off. Be encouraged though. While this will be a large number, effective implementation of the six steps to get out debt will calculate a revised number that will encourage you. You will pay a much smaller amount of interest if you remain focused on your vision and goals.

YOUR SPENDING PLAN CD – INSTRUCTIONS

1. Install your spending plan CD into your computer's CD drive and follow the setup instructions.

Note: Be sure to read the user documentation in the "Help" section and follow the setup instructions. If you have Windows 2000 or XP, the CD will load easily; just follow the prompts. After installation, you should see a gold coin icon on your desktop named "Fire Your Debt."

Double click on the Fire Your Debt icon.

2. In the upper left corner, click on **Vision and Goals > Overview**.
Enter your Vision Statement and read the formula for success and God's promises in Proverbs 3:9.

3. Click on the Short-Term Goals button. Enter your information. Now, review these goals and place them in priority order. I encourage you to make emergency fund priority number 1, if you don't have at least $1,000 in the bank for emergencies. Now click Close.

4. Click on the Long-Term Goals. Enter your information also insuring priority order and click Close.

STEP 2 – CREATE A NET WORTH STATEMENT

Your Assets –
Your Debts =
Your Net Worth Statement

LIST ALL YOUR ASSETS

As we learned in Chapter 3, you are a steward of God's resources. Stewards know the status of their possessions. In Job chapter 1:1, God begins by telling us who Job is. In verse 2, He tells us how many sons and daughters he has. And in verse 3, God gives us Job's net worth. God is a God of specifics, He lists everything. Therefore, the first thing I want you to do is list all your assets on a separate sheet of paper. An asset is what you own and a debt is what you owe.

1. Click on **Income and Expenses > Net Worth**. The Net Worth screen appears.

NOTE -- VERY IMPORTANT: Make sure the start date in the upper-right-hand corner is your first payday of the next full first month.

2. Enter the cash value amount you have accumulated in each category. Notice all the names of the categories can be changed to your assets and debts.

3. Notice, there are two sections of assets defined here. One is called Liquid assets and the other Total assets. I like to refer to these as Total Liquid and Total Solid assets. The significance I want you to capture is you must be focused on both liquid and solid assets. Liquid assets are those that will fund your retirement and solid assets are the comforts of paid for possessions. Since many Americans have never developed this thought pattern, recently, the government developed a plan to allow Americans to reverse mortgage. Since, these people who seek a reverse mortgage weren't focused on the liquid assets, they find themselves in need of reversing their mortgage and in effect they are selling their home back to a mortgage company with interest to give them a fixed income stream to make ends meet.

The book of Job is 42 chapters long. Job goes through much travail through 41 chapters appearing to lose everything but his faith. God speaks to him in chapter 41 and now we enter the final chapter, 42. Job does an interesting thing in verse 10, he prays for the men who have been speaking defeat into his life. Immediately, God moves in Job's life; and in the same verse God says I made Job prosperous again and gave him twice as much as he had before. Every time God restores, he gives you more than you lost. Being a God of specifics, in verse 12, God gives you Job's revised net worth in detail by every asset.

Before I leave the book of Job, look at chapter 1 verse 2 again. It says Job had seven sons and three daughters. Notice, God tells you about Job's children before he gives you his net worth in verse 3. In Psalm 127:3 we read "Sons are a heritage from the Lord, children are a reward." Our greater asset is our heritage, our children; wealth is secondary thus mentioned in verse 3. Treasure your children and grandchildren. In my opinion, they are God's greatest gift. While we concentrate on money in this book, God's prosperity is much broader than just money. III John 2 "Beloved, I wish above all things that you prosper and be in good health, even as your soul prospers." KJV

As you list your assets, your liquid assets are directly inputted from your bank statements or your 401K plans. In the total asset side, you list the values of your automobiles, household goods, etc; these values are the current value of the item and not the purchased price. For example, you can determine the value of your car by going to www.kbb.com. Your furniture should be listed at a value you think you could sell it for. The life insurance is only used for any cash value of your life insurance. This applies for whole life policies, NOT for term life insurance policies. Your home's value is based on its current market value or tax value. Notice at the bottom of the screen, your net worth is being calculated every time you enter a number. After you complete your assets, go back to the top of the screen and click on **"Debts."**

> *Every time God restores, He gives you more than you lost.*

Debt is the second component of the net worth calculation. We've listed 15 possible credit card entries and 10 miscellaneous debt entries. Begin by changing the name of "Credit Card 1" to your credit card's name. Now enter the amount of debt, the interest rate and the monthly payment. Automatically, this will calculate the remaining months to pay off the debt and the interest you will pay. Repeat this step for each one of your credit cards.

Most people are seeing this debt in this form for the first time. Your credit card company probably wouldn't want you to see this. *They make money by keeping you in debt.* I hope this information encourages you. No matter what the length of time calculates, you now have facts to attack the debt. Continue listing each of your debts. Specifically, when you list your mortgage, enter the current mortgage balance, interest rate and for the monthly payment, only enter the principle and interest payment. Your mortgage is comprised of four expenses; principle, interest, taxes and insurance. The principle and interest are debt expenses and the taxes and insurance are living expenses. We will include the taxes and insurance in step four.

Notice there are also three columns that are green. If you have income in excess of expenses, known as available dollars, in step 4, you will learn how to apply these to your debts to accelerate the debt payoff. These green columns will update automatically as you proceed through step 4.

I want you to now look at two numbers. In the lower right hand corner is your networth. Perhaps this is the first time you have known this number. The importance is not what the number is but rather that this is a day of new beginnings. I encourage you to minimally update your net worth annually. Write this number down. In a year from now, recalculate and compare these numbers. It should increase. The six steps to get out of debt causes debt elimination, increasing your net worth. The second number I want you to calculate is the total of your debt plus the interest you owe. This is your real debt. This is the amount we are going to defeat. This is the amount that is standing between you and your job opening allowing you to hire wealth.

STEP 3 – BECOME "ALLERGIC" TO PLASTIC

A credit card only weighs about an ounce, but can become a very heavy burden if we allow it to control us. The ease of obtaining multiple credit cards coupled without discipline to only use these cards as a tool has caused most households in America to need a credit card to be their crutch to make the ends meet each month. Almost all Americans need an automobile for transportation, a home to live in but we don't need credit cards to live on. Without the ability to defer gratification, we have record numbers of credit cards in use today. If you are going to fire debt, you have to begin with a conviction that you will not charge on any credit cards again unless you can pay the balance off each month. You might be saying you can't do this because you have dug a deep hole and you need credit cards to provide the money you need to live on each month.

A good friend of mine, Todd Cunningham wrote in 2004 to say:

> I know I probably sound like a broken record, but I want to state once again what a positive influence you have been in our lives. Having paid the credit card debt off, we are now working on the home mortgage. God willing, we will have that paid off in 10 years or less.

Todd went home to the Lord in December 2005 at the age of 40. His instructions to his wife Lili were to contact me and get their spending plan adjusted. As of this writing, Lili and I have met three times. She not only has a new spending plan, but she has a retirement plan and their mortgage will be paid off in 10 years or less. Todd was a provider for his family while he was on earth and he planned for his family's success. He is an excellent example of good stewardship and a man who takes care of his family.

In 2000, I met with a couple who had 35 credit cards carrying a balance of almost $60,000. They were only paying the minimum on most of the cards. While it looked discouraging initially, I went through these six steps to get out of debt with them. The plan materialized and in three years 10 months, all 35 credit cards were paid off. This couple came back and gave me one of my favorite teaching tools. They punched a hole in the upper corner of each card and linked them together to a 10 foot chain. The chain represented the shackles they were under with this level of debt. Attachment of the cards to the chain represented the freedom they now had with no credit card debt. They not only paid them all off, they cancelled all of them to close the door of plasticitis.

In step 3, you must identify the habits you have developed by using credit cards. It is these habits that step 4 will address with a change allowing you to be cured of plasticitis. This step is much harder than step one and two but has a great reward for you if you succeed. Recognize, the only person standing between you and success is you. You have complete control of your victory to develop new habits to replace the plastic habit.

STEP 4 - CREATING THE SPENDING PLAN

In the CD in the Income and Expense section, you are now ready to go to the second level called Input Data. Entering this area, you find there are two sections; Income and Expense. Once again, please read the instruction material in the "Help" section.

You can change the name of any row to customize your plan. The income you enter should be your net or take home pay, not your gross pay. This is because we only want to calculate from your available pay. You must also input the rate of pay. Many people now receive weekly or bi-weekly paychecks. A person who gets paid bi-weekly will receive 26 paychecks per year. This means that in two months out of the year, they receive three checks and the remaining 10 months they receive two checks. Most people paid bi-weekly cannot tell you what happened with the extra check in the three check months. With a spending plan, it calculates all your three-check months allowing you to plan to use this money to accomplish your vision and goals. This is why it is emphasized as being very important in step 1 to enter this date as the first payday of the next full month. You don't want to enter a pay date in the middle of the month since it will only calculate half the month's pay but the full month's expenses.

As you enter your income, notice the bottom right block of the screen called over/under. This is your income minus your debt expenses you entered from the net worth debt section in step 2. Make sure you list all your income. An income tax refund rate of pay will be annual. The annual Expense field defaults to the month of December. Therefore, you will need to go into each year in the Yearly Data and move this number to the month you expect your refund to arrive. If you enter a quarterly income or expense, it defaults to the last month of the quarter. If this is not correct for your situation, you will update it in the Yearly Data section that will be discussed in the next few pages.

ENTERING DATA

Now go to the **Expense** field. The first two rows are named **Tithe and Offerings**. Remember, you can change the name of any row to customize the plan for you. In Malachi 3, God tells us we rob Him in the tithe and offerings. It is easy to see how to rob Him in the tithe. He is specific that He wants our first tenth. It actually belongs to Him. You *pay* the tithe and you give the offering. God also tells us in Leviticus 27:30, 31 that if we (spend) the tithe, He will require 20%. If you create a spending plan without the tithe and offerings included, you are taking one step forward and multiple steps backwards. God is bound by

His covenant. Being a person who tithes and gives offerings are the foundation for you doing your part of God's covenant. God has already done His part.

Many times people ask me if they should tithe on the gross or the net pay. The tithe is from your gross pay. Did you know that America has only had "gross" and "net" pay for about 70 years? Before 1935, our government did not have debt. Americans received a gross paycheck and took care of our taxes at the end of the year. Then, in 1935, the current system of with holding taxes was put into place.

> *Remember this: Whoever sows sparingly will also reap sparingly, and whoever sows generously will also reap generously.*
> *— 2 Corinthians 9:6 NIV*

The offering is meant to be given over and above the tithe. God's laws of sowing and reaping have existed since Genesis 8:22, where He first teaches them. The tithe belongs to God. It is like an insurance policy. The insurance policy protects your assets and provides a base coverage for you. The offering, on the other hand, is what we give God. The offering allows us to receive the reaping. The offering is seed in the ground. Without seed in the ground, there will not be a harvest. In Mark 4:8, Jesus speaks of the parable of the sower. He said that seed fell on good ground and sprung forth some 30, some 60 and some 100 fold increase. The offering allows the exponential return of God to manifest in our lives.

Next, enter your remaining rows of expenses by name, rate of pay, and amount. Each time you enter a debt, watch the **Over/Under** column to make sure you still have a positive number. If your expenses exceed your income, this column's color changes to red. Make sure you input every debt expense and living expense. It is important to answer this question. Have you listed all expenses that you previously charged on a credit card? By doing this, you are stating that you are going to pay forward for these items now and the credit cards will not be added to allowing you to pay them off without making any additional charges.

PREPARE FOR THE POSSIBILITIES

I always encourage people to create an emergency fund. This should be their immediate, short-term goal. An emergency fund is for unexpected expenses. Usually, it is for a broken household item such as a dishwasher, perhaps car repair, or possibly an insurance deductible. You can also use an emergency fund to replace your salary if you lose your job or are laid off. Most people are not prepared for an emergency. Many budgets fail because they only plan for one month at a time. If an unexpected bill occurs and there is no savings, people are forced back into the use of credit.

I encourage people to build an emergency fund in a two-step process. 1) Accumulate $1,000 in funds. Then, begin to attack debt. 2) After you get your high-interest debts paid off, now set aside another month of emergency funds. Your goal is to build up your emergency fund so that it covers 3-6 months of living expenses. It's better to have it and not need it than need it and not have it.

A couple wrote me recently with this testimony:

> We just want to thank you again. We are still working with envelopes the way you taught us and try to stay in control with the spending plan. My husband lost his job recently when the company relocated. But thanks to your time and preparation, we are OK. We are looking forward to our next plan. We hope that after this season of change, we can personally thank you for helping us to have no fear in our hearts.

The key to success for this couple was they were prepared. I will discuss the envelop system later in this chapter. Notice, the positive attitude communicated by this couple. Also notice, as soon as he found a new job, they would begin re-planning the money by creating a revised plan based upon his new salary.

Before you exit the **Expense** section, please review the template below. Make sure you have comprehended every possible expense.

Spending Plan Model for your gross pay

TITHE	10%			
TAXES	25%		Insurance	Birthday gifts
F		Mortgage	Doctors	Graduation gifts
		Automobile	Dentists	Wedding/shower gifts
A		Food	Deductibles	Christmas gifts
M		Utilities	Teen cash	Seasonal decorations
	40%	Gasoline	Oil changes	Home repairs
I		Restaurants	Car repairs	Wedding
		Telephone	Cell phone	College
L		Cable/Internet	Cleaners	Retirement
Y			Medicine	New toys
			Clothes	Vacation
				Life Insurance
GIVING	5%			
SAVING	20%			

Now, you are ready to close the **Input Data** field.

1. Go back to the home page of the Fire Your Debt spending plan.

2. From the main menu, click on **Income and Expenses>Yearly Data**. Yearly Data is the last item on the drop-down menu.

3. The year you entered as your start date in the net worth page displays. The dates continue for six years.

4. You will see these six years listed across the top. The last item displayed is **Monthly Check**.

The only items listed are the items you entered in the net worth debt page and **Input Data**. It is also now listed in alphabetical order. People just starting their spending plans sometimes don't enter any numbers in the emergency fund or next car fund. I suggest you close out of the menu and go back to input data. Go to **Expenses** and find the rows named emergency fund and next car fund. Enter $1 in each of these two rows and then zero out the $1. You have now added these two rows to the yearly data report. When you are ready to direct funds to those categories, this serves as a placeholder row in the **Yearly** data for the time you can begin to fund these items.

The first cursory view of your **Yearly** data is the **Over/Under** row. All these numbers must be black and not red. If you have any red numbers, moving numbers around will accommodate a color change to black. An example of a number that could be moved might be clothing. If you planned $1800 a year for clothing and you entered $150 a month, you can move around available dollars to balance your over/under.

Notice that if you had a debt listed in the net worth sheet and it showed it would be paid off in 25 months. Scroll 25 months out into the **Yearly** data and you will see this debt's final payment to the penny. Notice, in the first year, the box in the lower right corner called **Debt Adjuster**. The letters are dark. You will need to go through all six years and insure your months are all in the black in order to get the letters **Debt Adjuster** to turn white.

Now you are ready to accelerate your debt payoffs. Once you enter **Debt Adjuster**, it displays all your net worth debts and your available dollars from the **Yearly** data. Select the debt you wish to pay off first and click payoff. Instantly, the available dollars were all moved to that debt. Instantly, the last three (green) columns of your net worth debt are filled The **Yearly** data fills in as well. When this debt is paid off, the monthly payment you were making is now available in the **Over/Under** field. Now, verify you have remaining dollars available in the **Over/Under** column. If so, then pay off your second debt and continue to do so as long as you have available dollars. (Once again, all numbers, in all years, listed in the Over/Under must be black and not red before you use Debt Adjuster)

Once you used all your available dollars, go back to **Yearly** data and notice the numbers in the **Over/Under** field are all $0. What you are doing is naming every dollar. As a steward of God, you are telling your money where it is going to go. You are now becoming the employer and your money is becoming your employees. You are now controlling your destiny.

To view the dollar amount of the victory, go back to net worth debt and look at the green column. It shows the revised months of debt, the revised dollars interest you will pay and your interest savings. How does this interest savings compare to your liquid net worth?

HANDLING MONTHLY PAY PERIODS

Since most people do not get paid monthly, we need a spending plan by paycheck. The **Monthly Check** field does this for you.

The **Monthly Check** field helps you break down your monthly spending into a "by check" plan. This process might take a little while. You must review each expense individually and determine when the bill is due (first check or second check). The system is set up to handle as many as five check periods, as needed, to accommodate people who are paid weekly.

Process:
The first thing you do is load the by check income by period. Notice on the right there is a check column that insures you have the same number totaled as the monthly plan did. Second step is to determine when a bill is due per pay period. If the auto insurance, for

example, is due the 22nd of the month, you would place it in the second check column and zero out the first check amount. Notice the checkbox called **"Cash."** Use this column for your envelope system. This is where you can make a variable cost a fixed cost. If you check this box, it adds the money to the cash row at the bottom. When you finish, you have a balanced by check, expenses equal income, and then there is a cash total. This is how much cash you should cash a check for and put it in labeled envelopes according to each expense type that was checked.

Envelope System:

I strongly advocate using the envelope system. Total your expenses in the **Expense** field for your next pay period. Get a box of plain white business mailing envelopes and label each one with one of your expenses, like "Groceries," "Gasoline," "Entertainment," etc. When you receive your paycheck, go to your bank and deduct the cash amount that equals that total. By putting cash aside in an envelope for each variable expense, you take control of each expense in your plan. If there's an item you don't want to use an envelope for, just remove the check mark. (Note: this description is also on the software program under the "Support" section.)

STEP 5 – DISCIPLINE

And have you quite forgotten the encouraging words I spoke to you, his child? He said, "My son, don't be angry when the Lord punishes you. Don't be discouraged when he has to show you where you are wrong. 6 For when he punishes you, it proves that he loves you. When he whips you, it proves you are really his child."
— Hebrews 12:5-6 TLB

Many times when I complete step 4 the person is excited. They can see much broader the road to victory. Most, for the first time, can actually see a financial vision of victory. I encourage them and tell them this was the easy part. The rest is

> *The only person standing between you and success is you.*

dependent upon their conviction towards success. They must develop new habits that allow the spending plan to work in their lives. Any time you have a change in your finances, a pay raise, a bonus, extra overtime, or anything else, your first thought should be to replan. The income section should be conservative as we never allowed for a pay increase. I encourage you to always have a strategy for increase. This strategy will be discussed in greater detail in Chapter 6. You will receive increases. Put God first with the tithe and the remaining increase should be applied to your goals, and then you will exit Debt City even faster than what this plan indicates.

God has a plan and a future for you. You can overcome debt. You can become the victor and not be the victim any longer. Now that you can see it, you should become passionate about firing debt. It will require discipline. Proverbs 10:4 God tells us the hand of the diligent will prosper. By being diligent in the implementation of the spending plan, you are firing debt. God tells us this is a prerequisite for prospering.

STEP 6 – CONDUCT A FAMILY MEETING
How can two walk together except they agree?
— Amos 3:3 KJV

For order and harmony to exist in your home, everyone living in your house should be in agreement with your spending plan. If you are married or engaged, sit down with your spouse or fiancé to discuss your joint financial vision. If you are a single person, I encourage you to get in agreement with *yourself or have a mentor to hold you accountable.* Your singleness does not exclude you from God's blessing or His provision.

> *Train up a child in the way he should go: and when he is old, he will not depart from it.*
> *— Proverbs 22:6 KJV*

You can't delegate teaching your children financial principles to someone else. I mentioned earlier, our schools don't teach them how to manage money. They will learn not by what you tell them but more by what you do. In this meeting you are declaring to them your new process. You speak to them in terms they can understand. My first time to do this with my children was in 1980. My daughters were ages eight and three. I explained what we were going to do and then I gave each of them three glass jars. One jar was labeled God, one labeled bank and the third labeled store. We gave them an allowance of $1 a week paid in dimes. We also allowed opportunities to make more money if they exceeded their duties that were required to obtain their allowance. By paying in dimes, the first dime went to the God jar, the next five dimes went to the bank jar and last four dimes went to the Store jar. I knew if I taught them to tithe and save as eight and three year olds, it would become a habit for them when they became adults.

Here's how to explain the envelope system to an eight-year old and a three year old: "We're going to buy things only when we have cash. We have several envelopes, each for a particular item. Groceries, for example, will be used every time we go to the grocery store. If we have money in the grocery envelope, we can buy our groceries. But if we run out of money, we won't go to the grocery store until the next payday, when we add the planned grocery money to this envelope. If you are at the check out and your child begins to beg for an item at the check out area, remind them the grocery envelop is for groceries. You can also ask them for their idea for a solution to allow the

> *Get in agreement with yourself.*

purchase next time you shop. What you have accomplished is explaining to your child, the problem is the amount of money or lack thereof in the grocery envelop, the parent isn't the problem. Conflict now exists between the child and the groceries envelope and doesn't manifest between parent and child. This presents what I call a teachable moment.

Be encouraged and passionate about these six steps to get out of debt. *It will work* and provide the path for you to know the month and year that debt will be fired.

In Chapter 5, you learn how to use your abilities to produce wealth.

EXPECTATIONS

1. I will write out my financial vision.
2. I understand that attack does not mean defeat.
3. I will check my heart to get rid of any unbelief that I can fire debt.
4. I am ready to learn how to use my abilities to build wealth.
5. The math is already coded in the software. I will not need to know difficult calculations to be successful.
6. I will walk in financial discipline and replan my spending plan whenever a change occurs.

5

USING YOUR ABILITIES TO PRODUCE WEALTH

But remember the LORD your God, for it is he who gives you the ability to produce wealth, and so confirms his covenant, which he swore to your forefathers, as it is today.
— Deuteronomy 8:18 NIV

The majority of Americans, if asked the question, "Do you want to acquire wealth?" would answer with a resounding YES. But if the next question was, "Are you actively planning to acquire wealth in your savings and investments?" sadly, the majority of Americans would answer no.

Many Christians want God to give them wealth, but never realize the answer to wealth is provided in one key word of Deuteronomy 8:18. God said He gives you the *ability*-- the ability to produce wealth. We tend to read the covenant promise of wealth and lay claim to it. Instead, I want to

> *What abilities are in your hand that you are running from?*

encourage you to lay claim on your abilities, then concentrate on the production of the abilities that will be transformed into wealth. In Chapter 3 we discussed developing your financial vision. Now, I'm challenging you to take an inventory of your abilities. I like to compare our abilities to tools in a tool box. You may be surprised to discover that abilities you already have could be used as wealth-building tools. For example, your hobbies, interests, passions or skills could be refined and directed to generate income. Your abilities could be the solution to someone's problem.

> *And the Lord said to him, What is that in your hand? And he said, A rod.*
> *And He said, Cast it on the ground. And he did so and it became a serpent [the*
> *symbol of royal and divine power worn on the crown of the Pharaohs]; and*
> *Moses fled from before it.*
> *— Exodus 2:2-3 NIV*

When God called Moses to be the leader of the Israelites, Moses protested his new job assignment, saying his skills were inadequate. God challenged him to use what was in his hand. To Moses' surprise, his hand held not just a shepherd's staff, but a symbol of leadership and power. Instead of embracing his gift, Moses ran from it. What abilities, what tools, are in your hand that you are running from?

WHAT'S IN YOUR TOOL BOX?

It's much easier to accomplish a task if you start with the correct tools. Imagine a carpenter going to work each day without a hammer and a square. It's even better when your tools are sharpened, polished and ready to use. Sometimes we show up for life each day without our tools, our abilities, polished and ready. Become a master of your abilities. God said He had a plan for us in Jeremiah 29:11. He continues by telling us it is a good plan, a plan to succeed. God has done His part. We do our part by using what we have in our tool box and continuing to acquire more tools. Fill your tool box with the

> **Become a master of your abilities.**

best tools. Practice using your abilities so that you are prepared when your time comes. Then, use your tools to produce excellent results for God. As you use your tools, always clean them up after use and put them back in their proper place. Then, when you need them again, like the five-talent servant in Matthew 25, they are ready to be put to use. As you use your abilities, perform all of your work in excellence. Never give a half-hearted effort when you are working towards your vision, your employer, your family or church.

TRUE BIBLICAL PROSPERITY

Churches will teach you to tithe and give offerings. However, by and large, the Church is not teaching believers how and why to acquire wealth. Many churches teach you to give, but what we will learn in the remainder of this book is how to harvest. It is true; you need to give in order to experience a harvest. You need seed in the ground to produce an exponential harvest. Your offerings are your financial seed. Now is the time to begin your harvest. In order to plant seed, you must have an open hand. If you close your hand and quit planting, God can not put something into a closed hand.

> *Feed your soul with God's Word.*
>
> *A debt-free believer can freely sow in to the Kingdom of God.*

On one end of the spectrum, some pastors discourage wealth-building as being worldly, invoking Jesus' words in Matthew 19:24: "it is easier for a camel to go through the eye of a needle than for a rich man to go into the kingdom of heaven." Additionally, some so-called "television prosperity preachers" tell us that if we simply send in a certain amount of money, we will experience supernatural increase (and get a free product).

What is the real answer? It is in God's Word. I encourage you to feed your soul with God's Word to find the truth. One thing is true when it comes to money: it is much needed – in the local church, in the Body of Christ and in the world's financial system. Over the past several years, sadly, there have been a small number of pastors or television evangelists who have misused money. When this occurs, the national media descends on the situation and it becomes visible to the world. However, let's not assume that because of the misconduct of a few, that God's instructions to pastors to manage the money entrusted to them via tithes and offerings is not valid. It is our responsibility to tithe to our church; it is the pastor's responsibility to use this money as if they were working for the Lord. We only hurt ourselves when we hold back because of other pastor's errors or we have a concern about tithing and giving and what the money will be used for.

To be clear: the tithe, all of it, belongs to your local church where you are fed the Word of God. The offering, anything above the tithe, can go where you see good soil (fruitfulness).

That could be in your local church, or it could be used to support worthy charities. It can also be given to an individual in need. Perhaps, God is allowing you to be part of a miracle in someone's life. After you pay tithes and give offerings, then begin to save from each paycheck. That's where your prosperity starts. Your savings receives the exponential return from God because you honored Him first. Whatever you do, stay in financial covenant with God. He will bless your faithfulness. (Please review the spending plan template in chapter 4).

The proportion of U.S. households that tithed their incomes to their churches dropped from eight percent of adults in 2001 to three percent in 2002. I have prepared spending plans for people who stopped tithing because of heavy debt loads. They usually declare their intent to make tithing a priority once they understand its importance. It concerns me as I create spending plans for people and they are more upset at having a bad credit report than having a bad tithing report. The tithe belongs to God. If you want to be a financial covenant partner with God, start by bringing your tithes to your church.

Why does God want us to use our abilities to acquire wealth? In Proverbs 13:22 he tells us a good man leaves an inheritance to his children's children. That is one reason. Another reason is in Acts 1:8. Jesus tells us we are to be witnesses in Jerusalem, Judea and Samaria and the rest of the world. We accomplish this through many ways, including funding the travel of missionaries and evangelists and other relief programs; television and radio broadcasts and even the Internet. It takes money to do all of that. Before the return of Jesus, all people on earth must have an opportunity to hear about Jesus. It takes money for this to occur.

God also tells us to give to the widows, orphans, and the poor. There are many scriptures to support this. God is waiting for you to do these good works. There is not a shortage of needs in this world. Nor is there a shortage of money. Eighty percent of the world's evangelical wealth is in North America. What *is* in short supply are five-talent Christians, mentioned in Matthew 25, to break America's debt cycle. God wants us to be debt-free so that we can freely give and sow money into the Kingdom and into our own investments, leaving a legacy for coming generations. This in turn now allows God to give back to you because a person who sows will reap.

DEVELOPING A MILLIONAIRE MENTALITY

Some of the richest people in the history of America started with nothing: L.J. Letourneau, Bill Gates, Michael Dell, Paul Allen, Steve Jobs, Oprah Winfrey. They all had one thing in common. They began with nothing and used their abilities to produce wealth. However, they didn't do this without a vision. Once again, Proverbs 29:18 tells us that God's people perish for lack of a vision. Dr. C. Thomas Anderson, in his book, *Becoming a Millionaire God's Way,* defines vision as "… being able to see the possible, unhindered by the past. It is the ability to look past the obvious and see the opportunity." Dr. Anderson is referring to seizing the opportunity to use your abilities to produce wealth. Both Abraham and Joseph used their abilities in the book of Genesis. There are men and women listed throughout the Bible who did so.

To develop a millionaire mentality, you have to delete the negative files in your belief system. Romans 12:2 tell us to be transformed by the renewing of our minds. Change is reinforced by what we REALLY think, say and do about our situations. Change in life is one thing that is guaranteed. Change occurs whether we want it to

> *Delete the negative files in your belief system.*
>
> *Begin thinking like a millionaire!*

or not. It's up to us to decide whether to go with the change, resist the change or become change leaders. We then replace the negative lies with Biblical financial truths. This causes positive thoughts, positive attitudes and positive words to come forth.

In the book of Exodus, the Bible records that after 430 years of slavery in Egypt, God's children were delivered and set free. They experienced many miracles, but still remained disobedient. They wandered in the wilderness for 40 years. When the Israelites finally left Egypt, they were physically free but they still had a slavery mentality. *Debt, You're Fired* gives you steps and processes to become physically free. However, total freedom comes when you set your mind to victory. Start purging your thoughts of the slavery mentality that results from debt. Begin thinking like a millionaire, not a poor person.

BIBLICAL FINANCIAL TRUTHS VS. THE WORLD'S LIES

Biblical financial truths	World's financial lies
You should be the lender	Borrow now with no payments for one year
You will reap what you sow	Buy now; pay later with interest
Leave an inheritance to your grandchildren	I am spending my children's inheritance
A sinner's wealth is stored up for the righteous	Spend, spend, and spend
Give and it shall be given to you	Live for today; que sera, sera
You're an heir according to God's covenant	It's every person for themselves
No weapon formed against you will prosper	Don't trust anyone; stay on the defensive
I wish above all things that you prosper	You're on your own. Only a few achieve success.

WALK OUT OF THE WILDERNESS

If you don't eliminate the Debt City mentality, you will stay in slavery and continually wandering in the wilderness of poverty. When you do this, you are not operating to a vision. As we previously stated, without a vision, people perish. You will always live paycheck to paycheck if you spend more than you earn. That is wilderness thinking. It will not work. The good news is you can eliminate wilderness thinking right now. In Chapter 4, you learned six steps to get out of debt and stay out of debt. Once you fire debt, you will never want to hire it again. If you do, you delay or eliminate the opportunity to hire wealth.

> *You can eliminate wilderness thinking.*

To paraphrase Sir Winston Churchill: "Never Give In" Take control of your life by working to walk out of the wilderness and walk in discipline. Our *Fire Your Debt* spending plan CD helps you begin to increase your financial abilities.

SUPPLEMENTING YOUR SHORTCOMINGS

It's better to have a partner than go it alone. Share the work, share the wealth. And if one falls down, the other helps, But if there's no one to help, tough!
— Ecclesiastes 4:9-10 MSG

No one knows how to do everything perfectly. If we did, we wouldn't need each other. I recommend finding a money mentor or taking a class to enhance the tools in your ability tool box. Our God's Money Man program pairs you with an FBC to walk with you throughout your debt-firing process. We also bring seminars to your city so you can learn how to master your money.

Seek the support of friends who support your goals. Bartering is a great way to accomplish your goals, and also a great way to get connected with people who support your vision. For example, if you know how to write a business plan, and your friend knows how to set up accounting books, perhaps you can help each other in your debt-firing quest.

DON'T BE DETERRED BY YOUR DEFEATS

A Super Bowl football team can be behind the entire game, and yet score a touchdown or field goal in the final few seconds to win. Next year, all people remember is *who* won, not *how* they won. Some fans will even struggle to remember the name of the runner-up team. So, when you lose a battle, see it as a temporary defeat. Re-plan, re-group and prepare to win the next battle. Focus on the score at the end of the game. Whoever wins the last battle is declared the victor. This is why Paul tells us in the New Testament that when we run the race, we run it to win.

> *When you lose a battle, see it as a temporary defeat.*

There is a battle line being drawn in the sand in this financial war. Most people would be happy just to get to "Broke." Getting to "Broke" means you have no debt – but you also have no assets. In other words, at this point in your financial life you have conquered debt but you can go much higher with savings and investing. Getting to broke doesn't win the financial battle. It is not the place God has provided for us in His covenant. He tells us He has pleasure in our prosperity, that we should be prosperous and have good health. Over the past generation, the average person spends more than they make and is losing the financial battle. It's time to build your financial ark. Prepare to be protected no matter how severe the storm is. It's time to start looking for the rainbow of God's financial covenant. Begin with a vision, a desire, and a declaration: Debt is your enemy. Declare war on all types of debt.

BECOME A FIVE-TALENT CHRISTIAN

God is looking for you to use your talents for Him. In Matthew 25 (the parable of the talents), Jesus mentions three servants. The master of these three trusted each one of them. But the Bible says he gave one person five talents, another two talents and the other one talent, each according to their abilities. How did one achieve more abilities than the other? Continue reading about the one that was given five talents. Matthew 25:16 tells us that the man who had received the five talents went at once and put his money to work and gained five more.

Here is a great example of using your abilities to produce wealth. The servant with the five talents didn't wait; he went immediately to work and doubled his master's money. A five-talent Christian uses his or her abilities to produce wealth. Your challenge is to set your mind towards victory. Strive to be a five-talent Christian in all you do. Don't hesitate – go immediately and use your talents.

THE POWER OF PARTNERSHIP

Many years ago, I saw a bumper sticker that read, "If God said it and I believe it, that settles it." When we partner with God, all things are possible – including miraculous debt elimination. We see this occur with the widow of Zarephath in 1 Kings 17. We see it again with a widow in 2 Kings 4 and several other places in the Bible.

> *Begin looking at your finances as a partnership with God.*

Businesses recognize the power of partnership in a relationship with supplier and customer. Marriages recognize the power of partnership when husband and wife are united. Churches recognize the power of partnership when the congregation captures the vision of the pastor. Parents recognize the power of partnership with their children, when they devote time to train them and stay involved in their lives. Today's billion-dollar businesses did not begin as billion dollar businesses. They grew and developed partnerships. To be successful, they needed successful partnerships. To have successful partnerships, every employee must communicate the company's vision as one voice to their suppliers and customers.

If you are married, the Power of Partnership must be applied to your family unit. A married person cannot have a separate vision and goals from their spouse. If you are single, communicate your vision and goals to friends who not only support your vision, but also are working to fire debt and hire wealth. Communicating your vision to someone who is not a committed debt-firer opens the door for them to speak defeat in your plans. They will tell you your vision is impossible. How will you ever have enough money to pay cash for a car, let alone, a home? Control your environment by only partnering with people of like minded financial vision and goals.

I want to encourage you to begin looking at your finances as a partnership with God. Colossians 3:23-25 reads: "Work hard and cheerfully at all you do, just as though you were working for the Lord and not merely for your masters, remembering that it is the Lord Christ who is going to pay you, giving you your full portion of all he owns. He is the one you are really working for. And if you don't do your best for Him, He will pay you in a way that you won't like-for he has no special favorites who can get away with shirking." (TLB) When you use your abilities to honor your Ultimate Partner, God, you will walk in excellence.

WHAT CIRCLE ARE YOU STANDING IN?

Jesus saith unto him, Rise, take up thy bed, and walk.
— John 5:8 KJV

You might be saying at this point; you just don't understand my circumstances. The word circumstance originates from two words: circle and standing. In other words, your circumstances exist because of the circle you are standing in. To change your circumstances, you have to do one of three things: 1) get *out* of your circle; 2) get *someone* out of your circle, or 3) invite someone *into* your circle. It is not our circumstances that cause us to get down about debt; it is our attitude towards those circumstances. You accept what you tolerate. In John 5, a man lay next to the pool of Bethesda for 38 years waiting to get into the water first so he could be healed. Because of the man's affliction, whenever the angel troubled the water, others always made their way ahead of him. But after 38 years of waiting, Jesus walks into the man's circumstances. Jesus told him to pick up his mat and walk. Because Jesus walked into this man's circle, in an instant his circumstances changed.

People generally earn within 20 percent of the people in their immediate circle of friends. Misery loves company. Perhaps you are being influenced by people who have no desire to see you fire debt or hire wealth. What are the people in your circle saying about your circumstances? As you work to accomplish your goals, you may find that you are standing in the wrong circle. If you want to become a millionaire, why are you hanging around with people making $20,000 a year?

Your thoughts will determine your attitude and subsequently, your words. Control your thoughts and you will develop a good attitude and speak positive words. Life is a daily learning experience. What we do with these experiences will determine how we improve our abilities. You are the only person standing between your past failures and your success-filled future. Every day we have choices that we can control. We can choose to be happy or sad. We can choose to be depressed or to have joy. Be like Joshua who said "as for me and my house, we will serve the Lord." Develop thoughts that draw from your current abilities. Next, develop a positive attitude that no matter what comes against you, you will learn from life daily and improve your abilities. Finally, speak these thoughts over your life and vision; stay focused and stay positive.

Jesus said in John 10:10 that He came so that we would have life and have it to the full. Living in debt is not living life to the full. Debt limits the growth of your abilities since you are using your talent to pay for another company's vision. When you decide to fire debt, I encourage you to develop your borders and establish boundaries. Life is a giant canvas that allows us to paint the picture. When debt enters in, it places a frame around our canvas. While it might be tolerable at first, since our frame might be an 11 by 14; the frame continually shrinks as more debt is accumulated. It shrinks to the point that the picture, or our vision, is not recognizable. John 8:32 says we will know the truth and the truth will set us free. The world's financial system doesn't want you to know the truth. They want you to fit into their criteria. Their criteria will limit your abilities. To increase your abilities, you must study to learn the truth. The implication in John 8:32 is that the truth you know will set you free. Truth is in God's word but you have to learn it and apply it to live life to the full.

A MARATHON, NOT A SPRINT

People come to our God's Money Man seminars after spending years and years getting themselves into financial bondage. They want God to get them out instantly, not realizing that debt-firing and wealth-hiring is a process. This is not a race against the clock or other people. This is longer than an actual marathon – this is a life journey. Once they realize that debt is spending tomorrow's wealth today and they can see objectively a plan to get out of debt versus remaining in the subjective area of just talking about debt, they can now attack debt. 1 Peter 5:8 from the Amplified Bible tells us to be well balanced and the enemy cannot devour you. The enemy would love to keep us in extremes. Excess is the enemy's playground. If you cannot manage the money you have today, how will you be able to manage more money tomorrow? A spending plan shows you, dollar by dollar, how to manage today's money to your vision and goals. It provides the financial balance that will place a hedge of protection around you prohibiting the enemy from devouring you. A balanced life of giving, living and savings will provide for you and your family today and in the years to come.

Abraham was the first rich man mentioned in the Bible in Genesis 13:2. God told him it was time to move. He didn't question God, he moved. Abraham was living amongst pagan friends and relatives. God wanted him away from all the negative talk and actions. Four chapters later, after being obedient to God's commands, God made his covenant with Abraham. What would you do if God told you to move? I want you to know He is telling you to move. He wants you to move out of the American system of debt to a land flowing with milk and honey. To do this, you have to focus on firing debt! When someone is fired from a job, they don't come back to work the next morning. They are forced to find other employment. This is how you need to look at debt. It is fired and is being removed, never to return again. This begins your balance in your financial life.

FINDING YOUR FINANCIAL MENTOR

Again, I tell you that if two of you on earth agree about anything you ask for, it will be done for you by my Father in heaven. 20 For where two or three come together in my name, there am I with them."
— Matthew 18:19-20 NIV

Words have power. I encourage you to have a financial mentor, who first, holds you accountable and responsible. Second, he or she should be allowed to encourage you and speak direction into your financial situation. You must, however, be very careful who you select for your mentor. It is good to develop a mentor relationship with a person who has already overcome debt and begun the process of accumulating wealth. Through God's favor, this person will come into your life. You must be patient and be silent concerning your vision and goals until you have a trusted mentor. Once you have this relationship, you must develop a servant's attitude. You must be open to teaching, instruction and discipline. In the long term, you will become successful more quickly by listening to a mentor. Then, years from now, you will become the mentor for someone just like you.

I have read dozens of financial books. The best one I have ever read is the Bible. It is a roadmap for success. The starting place for improving your abilities is in the Word of God. Pick up a Bible and begin reading God's plans and promises for you. In Galatians 3:29, God says that you are an heir of Jesus. You are special to Him. He created you as His masterpiece. You are unique. You were created to live today because he needs you to use your abilities to achieve the potential He created in you. God is not a respecter of persons. He loves you just like he loved Abraham, Isaac, Jacob, Joseph, David, Peter, James and John; and the list goes on. If a fisherman can put away his nets and immediately begin pursuing Jesus, so can you. When Peter, James and John put up their nets, they sought to follow Jesus. They started as followers, then they became leaders; later, they developed into five-talent Christians. They didn't make excuses when Jesus asked them to come with Him. They simply *went.* Increasing your abilities is easy. All you have to do is start with that expectation today. It is never too late to begin again.

The next chapter will teach you how to develop a strategy for increase that dramatically increases the size of your circle!

EXPECTATIONS

1. Today, I will take inventory of the abilities in my tool box.

2. Today, I will start practicing my abilities so they will be ready to use.

3. I will make giving tithes and offerings a priority in my debt-firing strategy.

4. I will begin thinking like a millionaire and take control of my thoughts and words.

5. I will look for ways to barter my abilities to accomplish my goals, and help others.

6. I will look for the right financial mentor to help me fire debt and hire wealth.

6

DEVELOPING A STRATEGY FOR INCREASE

But these things I plan won't happen right away. Slowly, steadily, surely, the time approaches when the vision will be fulfilled. If it seems slow, do not despair, for these things will surely come to pass. Just be patient! They will not be overdue a single day!
— *Habakkuk 2:3 TLB*

What do you want to achieve or avoid? The answers to this question are objectives. How will you go about achieving your desired results? The answer to this you can call strategy. – *William E Rothschild*

The Bible speaks of our words having life. What we say about a situation often determines its outcome. The words you use to describe your desired goals should describe the destination you desire; if you think you can or you think you can't, you're right.

What do you say about your life? This is important to decide as you develop your strategy for increase. Do you call yourself independent or dependent? Do you speak of yourself as wealthy before the fact, or do you despair, "I'm up to my eyeballs in debt!" Do you speak of the reward in a strategy, or do we decline an opportunity, saying, "That's just too risky."? One focuses on the positive outcome; the other on the negativity of the circumstances. Romans 4:17 says that God called those things that are not as though they were. He tells us to emulate His example. So, as you work out your God-given strategy for increase, we should verbally expect a positive outcome. If you are tithing and giving to God according to Malachi 3, He says you can test Him in the area of finances and see if He will not open up the floodgates of heaven. Can you take a moment and imagine what comes to you when God opens His floodgates? Expect it to happen if you are tithing and giving offerings.

The cornerstone of developing your strategy for increase is to understand that *you are in control*. You are the only person responsible for your financial future – not your employer, not your 401(k) plan administrator; not your boss; no one but you.

One of the biggest financial mistakes people make is depending on others to make choices for them. We depend on others to make our investment decisions, depend on the government to take care of us upon retirement; and we depend on our employer to provide lifetime income and benefits. Some of us depend on "quick-fix" debt-consolidation companies. There are companies today who will help you fire debt and there are also companies today who will help you hire wealth. However, remember two things: 1) a company exists to make a profit, and 2) if you hire a company to fire debt, you are giving them control and responsibility to fix your mistakes. If you don't take control in firing your debt, you won't understand the process of firing debt. It's likely you will wind up in the same situation in a few years. You also accrue additional debt in the form of fees paid to the consolidation company. But, if you use the six steps to get out of debt taught in Chapter 4, you take control of your debt. There is no better solution to firing debt than the old fashioned way – taking control of your own financial future and spend less than you make.

YOUR APPOINTED TIME TO INCREASE

There's an opportune time to do things, a right time for everything on the earth:
— Ecclesiastes 3:1 MSG

And now, GOD, do it again--
   bring rains to our drought-stricken lives
   So those who planted their crops in despair
   will shout hurrahs at the harvest,
   So those who went off with heavy hearts
   will come home laughing, with armloads of blessing.
   — Psalm 126:4-6 MSG

There are two Greek words in the New Testament that describe the concept of time. One, *kronos*, is where we get the word chronological. It refers to a specific segment of time, such as thirty minutes ago; next week. The word, *kairos*, refers to an appointed time, a set time ordained before the foundation of the world. When we hear people refer to "their season" this is the time they refer to. At this point, you have sown seeds into your financial future. You have courageously, perhaps tearfully, faced the consequences of your own decisions. You have committed yourself to becoming debt-free. You have learned to put God first by bringing the tithe. You have set the stage for increase by putting order into your home and into your finances. You have to put together a blueprint for success by using the software provided in this book. You went on a "debt diet" by placing yourself on a spending plan. Now, prepare yourself: It's your time! God's Word doesn't lie. God operates outside of the concept of time. Time is just for humans to measure the sequence of events. He promises, in due season, to reward your obedience to Him as a faithful steward over the resources, financial and otherwise, that He has blessed you with. Increase is promised. Seed time and Harvest time is a law from Genesis 8:22 just like gravity is a law. We all know gravity exists and respect it and do not jump off the roof. Through faith, you must capture that seed in the ground will bring a harvest as surely as gravity exists if you jump from a roof. If God said it, then no man can change it. Harvest is always a result that occurs after you have planted.

DO WHAT YOU CAN DO

The famous Serenity Prayer begins:

God grant me the serenity
to accept the things I cannot change;
courage to change the things I can;
and wisdom to know the difference.

An important component of financial security is learning to control the things you can control. You cannot control Social Security, your employer, taxes, inflation, or risk of single investments. You can, however, control your own spending, find alternative income sources, and implement methods to reduce your taxes; put away cash for retirement and maximizing investment potentials and diversification. But to achieve this level of control, you need to devote time to educating yourself in money matters. Some very informative web sites for people who want to learn about money and how it works are: MSNMoney. com, Motley Fool.com and especially the web site where you have your 401K plan or 403b plan. The more you educate yourself in money matters, the more weapons you have at your disposal in your wealth-building arsenal.

ACQUIRING WEALTH GOD'S WAY

We went through fire and flood. But you brought us to a place of great abundance.
— Psalm 66:12

The first step in the process of acquiring wealth God's way is applying a simple rule to your spending: 10-10-80. The first 10 is the 10% tithe. As we discussed before, God's Word teaches us that it is imperative to apply this first step to be in financial covenant with Him. Therefore, the tithe is the primary key for financial blessings from God. If we attempt to control our finances on our own, we do this with our natural abilities. The tithe invites God to become your financial partner. God brings His supernatural abilities to your finances. Now, when you combine the supernatural abilities of God with your natural abilities, the results will be miraculous.

However, simply giving the 10% tithe does not bring automatic success. The second step of the 10-10-80 rule is to pay yourself by beginning a saving process of 10% of your gross income. This means putting yourself and your family ahead of any other demand for your money. Deposit a set amount each and every payday. Are you taking advantage of your employer's 401K plan matching contributions? This second 10% is an excellent place to capture the benefit of free money that will enable your investments to grow much quicker. This money that you pay yourself should be for your future. This is your financial freedom vehicle. Without savings discipline, you lose control of future choices. Many people beginning their five-year spending plan say, there isn't any money left after paying their bills to save. That's one reason to set it aside first. I tell them to make a one-month detailed analysis of where they spent their money during a pay period. How many times did you stop for coffee or eat lunch out?

Look at the 10% savings as your employees. As your saving's employer, you define the job requirements. These employees have the job responsibility of working each and every day to ensure you have a comfortable, financially independent retirement. More than half of all Americans have no retirement savings. 60% of workers say they are behind schedule when it comes to planning and saving for retirement. If you direct your employees properly, you don't have to be one of those workers.

If you make saving a high priority, you will have money to save. Analyze where you spend your money and adjust it to the most important priority. Consider bringing your lunch to work, or substituting seeing a first-run movie for a "dollar" movie. You can use coupons for dining out, or plan your errands all at once to save gas. Step 2 is essential if you are going to take control and not be a dependent. A dependent has limited choices. An independent has choices. It is amazing to see how fast your savings will grow through compounded interest.

Being independent isn't a question of how much money you will earn over your lifetime. It is a question of how much you will save. If you average $11.11 an hour in your lifetime, you will make approximately $900,000 cumulative. If you made $11.11 an hour, a 10% savings would be $2,222 a year. After 40 years of this habit of saving, investing in stocks with an average annual return of 12%, you would accumulate $1.9 million or over twice what you made in your life time pay. Few of us apply this simple math to our long term view because we have not developed our debt-firing strategy. If you implement the 10/10/80 rule today and continue throughout your working life, you will have choices. Take control of your finances today. Save 10% of each and every paycheck and control the wants of life today. If you are in your thirties or older, you will most likely need to save more than 10% if you haven't begun your retirement savings and investing yet.

THREE STEPS TO FRUITFULNESS

In Genesis 1:28, God told man and woman to be fruitful, multiply and replenish the earth. After the flood in Genesis 9, God told Noah the same three things: Be fruitful, multiply and replenish the earth. You won't be able to retire comfortably just by savings and putting your money into a money market account or a certificate of deposit. These savings instruments pay interest that is at or below the rate of inflation. Over the past 50 years, the Standard & Poor's 500 stock has averaged 10.4% total return per year. Inflation over the same 50-year period has averaged 4.1%. Thus, stocks have produced a real rate of return of 6.3% per year over the past 50 years.

The three-step process is as follows:

- **Fruitful** – Saving 10% from each paycheck.
- **Multiply** – Begin investing to allow your money to multiply.
- **Replenish** – Giving back some of the multiplied money
  (this is your money seed for your next harvest)

I have always been a saver. I was blessed to have a wife, Carla, who is also a saver. Many times one spouse is a spender and the other a saver. Occasionally, both spouses are spenders. Here is how I saved money during the 10 years I worked at Texas Instruments before I came to Compaq. My friends would buy lunch from the company cafeteria each day. I would bring my lunch in a brown paper bag and save the difference in money from what they paid at the cafeteria. Using the 10.4% return we discussed earlier, the $100 a month I saved compounded to $100,000 in savings in 22 years. Over a 44-year work life, this $100 would actually grow to $977,000. It doesn't take a lot of money to begin. It does take discipline to continue to save from each payday and plant those money seeds into your future.

Please recognize that only saving 10% of your income will not automatically create a comfortable retirement. You must save the 10% and invest it intelligently, thus allowing you to receive the interest and dividends. The 10% is a rule of thumb number for people to achieve financial independence if they begin in the early 30's. The older you are when you begin this process, the larger percentage of savings you require to accelerate your retirement preparation. This will be covered in greater detail in Chapter 7. Once you have become debt free and created an emergency fund totaling your 3-6 months living expenses, then you are ready to begin the investment process.

FACTOR IN YOUR FUTURE

In 1985, Compaq Computer Corporation began their 401K plan. A good friend of mine was not going to put money into it. His excuse was, "I can't afford to put money into a 401K plan." In actuality, he couldn't afford NOT to start a plan. I persuaded him to fund his 401K plan. As a result, he was able to retire while still in his mid-50s. He thanked me for helping him make choices that resulted in his ability to retire early.

As part of your financial foundation, after establishing a liquid emergency fund, you should open and deposit funds into either a 401(k) plan or Roth IRA, or a combination of the two.

You can determine this balance equation by calculating the tax consequences that result from a mix of tax-free and tax-deferred investments. The following is a simple example comparing the two retirement choices:

401(K) Example	Roth IRA Example
Balance $1,000,000	Balance $1,000,000
Personal Income tax bracket 25%	Personal Income tax bracket 25%
Taxes due on 401K $250,000	Tax due on Roth $0

Saving into a 401K plan allows you to defer taxes until the time when you take distribution of your 401K plan. As of January 1, 2006, companies are now able to begin offering Roth 401K plans. As we progress through this decade, many more companies will allow the employees the choice of a 401K or a Roth 401K plan. The Roth 401K opportunity is available until December 31, 2010 unless Congress votes to extend it. I encourage you to analyze your comparison. A 401K plan will allow you a lower income tax bill today because the taxes are deferred. A Roth 401K is funded with after-tax dollars and grows tax free. This is where your "dollar employees" will multiply.

Most people living paycheck to paycheck believe that they can't afford to start a 401K plan. However, that money is tax-deferred. If a person is in a 25% tax bracket, for every dollar they save, their take home pay will only be reduced approximately 75 cents. In other words, you are delaying the payment of the taxes now allowing this money to totally work as your employees in your company's 401K plan. Your belief is also that your tax rate will be less than 25% when you begin to withdraw funds from your 401K plan.

SUCCESSFULLY SORTING YOUR SPENDING

What about the other 80%? This is the remaining money that your employer withholds in taxes and the amount remaining that you will use for all your living expenses including giving and debt payments. You might want to consider using the "envelope system" to handle the rest of your spending. In other words, withdraw a certain amount of cash for weekly expenses like gasoline and groceries. I don't automatically recommend using "auto-pay" automatic deductions from your checking account for this reason: if you forget to enter it in your check register, it could throw your entire account balance off. I only use it for my health insurance payment. For example, if you plan $300 a month for groceries, by only purchasing groceries from your grocery envelope money, you guarantee that you will not spend more than $300 a month for groceries.

NEEDS vs. WANTS

Adjust your lifestyle to long-term thinking. One tough rule of life is that you can't have everything. You have to make conscious decisions about your purchases. Take out a piece of paper and write out two columns labeled "Wants" and "Needs." Needs must be taken care of now. 1 Timothy 5:8 tells us a man must take care of his family. This means taking care of the needs. It doesn't have to include everything your children ask for. Ask yourself a simple question before each purchase: Is this a "need" or a "want?" You might not need a new car, but you might want it. You might not need a bigger house but you want one. You might not need that faster computer but you want one. If you can live out of the needs column today, you will have more ample choices in the "Wants" column later, when you are financially secure. Your up-front sacrifices might be tough initially, but will pay off in the form of wonderful long-term benefits that create a healthy, stress-free financial atmosphere.

TIME x MONEY = INDEPENDENCE

It doesn't matter where you have been. What matters today is where you are going. Complete this formula for yourself. Time is how many paychecks you have remaining in your working life. Money is the amount you will save from each paycheck, after the tithe. The independence comes from solving this equation for your own financial vision and goals in life. The responsibility is yours. Take control of your financial future today by making your money work for you! This exercise also provides a macro look at what can be saved cumulative over the remaining pay days of your working life.

4 M'S TO DEVELOP YOUR
STRATEGY FOR INCREASE

A certain ruler asked him, "Good teacher, what must I do to inherit eternal life?"

"Why do you call me good?" Jesus answered. "No one is good-except God alone. You know the commandments: 'Do not commit adultery, do not murder, do not steal, do not give false testimony, honor your father and mother.'"

"All these I have kept since I was a boy," he said.

When Jesus heard this, he said to him, "You still lack one thing. Sell everything you have and give to the poor, and you will have treasure in heaven. Then come, follow me."

When he heard this, he became very sad, because he was a man of great wealth. Jesus looked at him and said, "How hard it is for the rich to enter the kingdom of God!

Indeed, it is easier for a camel to go through the eye of a needle than for a rich man to enter the kingdom of God."
— Luke 18:18-25 NIV

Motives – Webster defines this as some inner drive, impulse or intention that causes a person to do something or act in a certain way. Review your vision and goals again and check them to this definition. In Luke 18:18-25 a young ruler of Jesus' time approached Him with the above question. Jesus' response exposed the ruler's motives. He told the man, "You still lack one thing. Sell everything you have and give it to the poor; (then) you will have treasure in heaven. This ruler was religious by the law. Unfortunately, the ruler's money owned him instead of the other way around. Jesus recognized how important money was to the ruler. His motives were so focused on what he had now that he missed what Jesus was offering to him. As you accumulate wealth, you always need to check your motives. This ruler went away very sad because he was so rich that his wealth controlled him. The man

> *No matter how much you have, God is always your source.*

didn't understand that when he gives to the poor, he was giving God an opportunity to exponentially give back to him, because he was now using his abilities for God.

I have heard many inaccurate sermons preached on this and other passages dealing with finance. It's been taught that this young man couldn't enter the kingdom of God because he was wealthy. Read the verses again. What manifests in some people as they accumulate wealth is a love for money. 1 Timothy 6:10 is often misquoted as "money is the root of all evil." In fact, it actually says the *love* of money is the root of all evil. Proper motives aligned with God's word keeps you focused on money as a seed for you to sow. Again, God doesn't mind us having possessions as long as they don't possess us.

> *Command those who are rich in this present world not to be arrogant nor to put their hope in wealth, which is so uncertain, but to put their hope in God, who richly provides us with everything for our enjoyment.*
> — *1 Timothy 6 17 NIV*

Notice again: God doesn't say it is bad or a sin to have wealth. He speaks clearly that the problem is the arrogance and hopes a person places on the wealth. Money is not your source, no matter how much you have stewardship over. *God is always your source.*

Jesus went on to say in Luke that it is easier for a camel to go through the eye of the needle than for a rich man to enter the Kingdom of God. Many sermons have used this verse to explain to their congregation that wealth is bad. 'You can't get to heaven if you are rich' is one interpretation. All you need to do is understand what Jesus is talking about when he compares the rich entering heaven to the camel going through the eye of the needle. A camel going through the eye of a needle is impossible. A rich person who places their money above God will find it impossible to enter the Kingdom of God. However, a rich person who assumes the role of steward of God's possessions will accumulate wealth for the Kingdom; he or she will sow and reap and become a giver for God. The difference is the motive of the person. Here is a good question to ask yourself as you move into your wealthy place and begin to accumulate wealth: Are you closer to God now than when you had debt?

Mentality – Webster defines this as your mental capacity. Has anyone ever used all their mental capacity? I don't think so. Search the Internet and you will find some states have defined mental capacity in their laws and wrote a policy on mental capacity for their country. What I find amazing is these laws are all written defining mental capacity in a degenerative sense; lacking mental capacity.

Today I challenge you to recognize you do not have a decreasing mental capacity if you continue to strive to learn. Every time you learn something new, your mental capacity increases. Every May, we read of senior citizens finally obtaining their college degree. To accomplish this, their mental capacity increased. Every time you read the Word of God, your faith increases. Mental capacity is a matter of filling your mind up with more than you forget. Read introductory books on how to invest. Learn how your investments are performing. Find out what the associated fees are that you may be paying for these investments. Remember, *you* are the steward of your investments. As you begin to increase your control over your investment performance, you will find that your mental capacity increases dramatically.

Mentors – Webster defines this as a teacher or coach. I encourage you to find yourself a financial mentor; a person who is able to teach you from experience the mechanics of money. I advocate a "one up, one down" mentoring process. The "one up" is your mentor, a person whom you allow to hold you accountable to your spending plan and your walk towards your vision. The mentor is also someone who has *already been successful* accomplishing where you desire to get to. You do not want a mentor who is up to his eyeballs in debt with no plan of action. You want a mentor who has become successful, who walks in integrity and has strong values.

This now allows you to become a mentor, thus the "one down" approach. As you increase your mental capacity via learnings from your mentor, you are becoming qualified to become a mentor for others in the future and you increase your abilities simultaneously. My dad mentored me in the area of money and investing. As I grew in knowledge, I began to mentor my daughters. Additionally, I have helped many people develop their own spending plans. Most of them were implementing this process for the first time. Some of these people have become proficient in finance and gone on to become a Financial Biblical Coach and teach others from their own positive experiences.

Multiplication – You now should desire to see multiplication of your savings, not just addition. In Job, we discussed the change in Job's assets listed in chapter 1:3. God doubled each asset in the final chapter 42:12; the multiplication effect was two. When David commented in 2 Samuel 12 about the man Nathan was describing he said, he should repay four times the loss. In Genesis chapter 1, God created man in his image. He says we have dominion and that he has given us the herb bearing seed. He then tells us to be fruitful, multiply and replenish the earth. Notice, he didn't tell us to *add* to the earth, but *multiply*. There is an exponential occurrence as you begin the multiplication process. Instead of multiplying b times b in a mathematical equation, you move to the algebraic equation of b times b times b or, b cubed. For example:

If b=2 (2 times 2 is four but 2 times 2 times 2 is 8, it is exponential)

In my previous lunch example of saving $100 a month, adding this money at the end of 22 years would result in $26,400. The multiplication through investing allowed it to grow 10.4% per year resulted in $100,000. It is the same amount saved but investing allowed for 278% more money after 22 years. The savings became exponential when I allowed the savings *plus* annual interest each year to join together causing a larger increase year after year. Every year you allow your investments to multiply gives you more choices in the future.

Your wealth multiplies when you are in financial covenant with God. To accomplish this, all you need to do is tithe, give offerings and be obedient to God's commandments. This allows God to move in your finances. The spending plan, supported by your vision and goals, gives you the foundation to become a good steward of God's resources. Always check your motives, mentality, mentors and multiplication. As you multiply, remember this is not your wealth; rather, you are managing this wealth for God.

Your net worth will be a measuring tool for you to begin to track your wealth you are managing for God. Once again, I encourage you to update your net worth at least yearly. Keep track of what changes occur. It gives you a beginning point for your financial testimony.

FIVE COMPONENTS OF A SUCCESSFUL STRATEGY FOR INCREASE

"For I know the plans I have for you," declares the LORD, "plans to prosper you and not to harm you, plans to give you hope and a future."
— Jeremiah 29:11 NIV

Does this Scripture sound like it comes from a God who wants to see you just barely get by in life? No, it states God's plans. He is declaring to YOU, "I have plans to prosper you and give you hope and a future." You are a champion for God. It doesn't take a lifetime to accomplish firing debt, but it does take a cause. Your cause should be stated in your vision statement. Change will occur in your finances when you change your attitude about debt. Debt is not your friend. Treat it like it is an enemy.

I hope you are obtaining knowledge and information in this book. But there is more. Knowledge reveals what is wrong in a situation. Wisdom reveals the solution. As you develop your strategies for increase, seek God's wisdom.

1. The spending plan is your process to fire debt. It should become your method of managing your paychecks to your vision and goals; it details specific time periods for payoff of each debt.

2. Develop your strategy for increase as soon as you complete your spending plan. It creates an attitude of expectation that the raises and bonuses will come. Since you did not plan for the raises and bonuses in your spending plan, your list for your strategy for increase will be your plan to know exactly what to do when the increases come. Successfully implementing Step 1 and 2 causes you to live in diligence. With a new strategy for increase in your spending plan, you will fire debt faster than the original plan.

3. As you become debt free, you now have additional money that previously was paid to a lender. Get excited – Now you are becoming the lender! Begin to study to learn where to invest this money.

4. Manage your investments and adjust your vision as you accumulate wealth. History records economic cycles. They are a guarantee. With wisdom and diligence, you will know when to move your investments according to the move in the economy. Some times it makes sense to own more stocks than bonds, sometimes more bonds than stocks, sometimes, it makes sense to not be in the market but on the sidelines in cash. You need to be in control and know the changing seasons; so no matter what is occurring in the economy, you have positioned your net worth to increase. Most of the time, you will need to be diversified between stocks, bonds and cash. I encourage you to complete an investor profile before you begin any investing. This profile will determine your diversification strategy based upon your tolerance for risk and your goals.

5. Forecast your future investment and saving growth. Monetarily, there is no better accelerator of hope than to see a forecast of what your money will multiply to over time. Our FireYourDebt.com site contains several calculators to help you manage your money. Many web sites for 401K plans have these calculators available as well. In this step, you become a strategist and not a tactician. A strategist is able to get above the paycheck to paycheck and see the big picture. Your big picture is determined by how well you accomplish these steps. History indicates America experiences a 3% inflation rate per year. Your strategy for increase must be adjusted for inflation and also the fees and commissions you pay for your investments. For example, if inflation is 3% and you pay 1.5% in fees and commissions and you want to realize an 8% return each year, you will roughly need your investments to grow 12.5% per year.

In Chapter 7, you will learn how you can plan for a successful retirement, no matter what stage in life you are in. More than 25% of the total workforce in the United States will reach retirement age by 2010. 62% will retire with less than $10,000 income per year. Will you be one of them? If you are behind on your retirement savings, don't despair: Chapter 7 will teach you how to catch up!

EXPECTATIONS

1. I will educate myself in money matters.
2. I will start an emergency fund that totals 3-6 months of my living expenses.
3. Once I have secured my emergency funds, I will begin the investment (multiplication) process.
4. As I develop my strategy for increase, I expect that raises and bonuses will come.
5. I recognize although people may be used to bless me, *God is always my source.*
6. As I prosper, I will look for God's direction where I can financially be a blessing to others.

7

RETIREMENT WITHOUT REGRETS

Wisdom is good with an inheritance: and by it there is profit to them that see the sun.
For wisdom is a defense, and money is a defense: but the excellency of knowledge is, that wisdom giveth life to them that have it.
— Ecclesiastes 7: 11-12 KJV

Retirement. What images and ideas appear when you read that word? This word has different meanings to different people. To some people, it means finally saying goodbye to the company, selling the family home and moving closer to the grandkids. For others, it means buying a recreational vehicle and chasing warmer climates. For some "empty nesters," it means enrolling in school or taking up that hobby they always were interested in. Unfortunately, for many Americans, retirement means...continuing to work. In 1999, the average Internet search engine revealed nearly a half million references to retirement. In 2006, there are 334 million. Americans have a rising obsession with the subject of retirement, but few know what to do to have a successful one. At retirement time, if you don't have enough money, it won't be because you did not earn enough money in your lifetime. It will be because you did not have a plan and invest wisely.

> **Think of your retirement as a "major purchase."**

THE FORMULA FOR A SUCCESSFUL RETIREMENT

A vision +

A disciplined plan =

A successful retirement

In 1978, Carla and I were in the process of buying our first home. A friend of mine said to us: "This will be the largest purchase you make in your life." That seemed to make sense to me; it sure was the largest at the time. Life has taught me the largest purchase we make in our lives is actually retirement, not our home. When you think about the costs of retirement years compounded by inflation, you learn that most people are retired a lot longer than they live in their homes. It doesn't take long to realize the need to plan, save and invest for this lifestyle change. In this chapter, I encourage you to think of retirement as a "major purchase." Just like your home has a monthly mortgage, you should purchase retirement with monthly installments. For as little as a $50 weekly investment earning 9% annual return, in 40 years you will accumulate $1,026,853. It doesn't take much to become a millionaire, but it does take a habit of saving and investing.

WORK TO RETIRE...OR RETIRE TO WORK?

A recent study by the Department of Health and Human Services uncovered some disturbing trends. For every 100 people starting their careers, by age 65 only four will be able to retire comfortably. 73 of those 100 will need to rely on others for support and 23 will need to continue working.

By contrast, 65 years ago in America, people didn't retire at all. During the 1940's, America had 132 million people, our nation's federal debt was only $43 billion, and the life expectancy for a man was 60.8 years. A woman's life expectancy was 68.2 years. In other words, most people didn't live long enough to have a lengthy retirement.

In 1900, the world life expectancy was approximately 30 years; fast forward to 1985. World life expectancy increased to 62 years. Life expectancy changes as you get older. By the time a child reaches their first year, their chances of living longer increase. By the time of late adulthood, our chances of survival to a very old age are quite good. For example, although the life expectancy from birth for all people in the United States is 77.7 years, those who live to age 65 will have an average of almost 18 additional years left to live, making their life expectancy almost 83 years.

Today, advances in medicines and physical fitness result in an increased life expectancy in America. Let's compare the years a person works to the years they will be retired. For example, a female born in 1927 might have gone to work at age 22 and worked until age 65. According to the above statistics, let's assume she dies at age 68.2. She worked 43 years and was retired for 3.2 years, which calculates her work to retirement ratio at 13.44. Compare this to the woman who was born in 1950. The health care report calculates males will now live to 74.5 years and females to 79.9 years for an average life expectancy in America of 77.7 years. The woman born in 1950 working until age 65 retires and lives until 79.9. Her work to retirement ratio is 2.88. This means for every 2.88 years she works, she needs to accumulate retirement funds for one year of retirement. The work-to-retirement ratio continues to decrease. This is why the majority of people living in the most prosperous country in the world can't afford to retire. However, you can have a prosperous retirement IF you become passionate about firing debt and hiring wealth -- regardless of your work-to-retirement ratio.

What does this data tell us? Obviously, we are living longer. That means we need more retirement savings and investments to bridge the time between retirement and "permanent retirement." Researchers who attempt to forecast the ceiling to how long people age have continually been proven wrong. The data reflects that the longevity of Americans increase three months for every year. Every four years, life expectancy increased by one year. That means that a child born in 2000 would have a life expectancy of 97. Now, if this child worked the same 43 years, retired at age 65, their ratio would be 1.34. (Note: 43 years worked divided by 32 years retired). Today, we have a greater chance of outliving our retirement savings than in any other generation.

As you can see, the ratio continues to decline. The child born in 2000 will work 1.34 years for every year they are retired. Compound this with an estimated 3% inflation. That child will need many more dollars to fund their retirement years than they made in their working years. This data means that we should prepare our children and grandchildren to be millionaires. A child born in 2000 and beyond will need more than a million dollars just to pay their bills at age 65. They will need several million dollars to leave an inheritance to their children's children. Being a millionaire is not a privilege, it is a choice. When you choose to be a millionaire, you increase your choices. As long as you *think* that becoming a millionaire is impossible, it will be impossible to you. We need to rid our minds of limited thinking. Think on the unlimited potential God has created in you. His Word tells us we can do *all things* through Christ who strengthens us.

Biblical ages in the Old Testament were much longer. Adam lived to be 930. Noah was 500 years old and then had three sons. Today, we are surprised to see a 50 to 60 year old parent with their newborn baby. God made this declaration in Genesis 6:3 "My Spirit will not contend with man forever, for he is mortal; his days will be a hundred and twenty years." (NIV) In other words, according to the Word of God, life expectancy *could* reach 120. Now apply this ratio. Work from age 22, retire at age 65 and die at age 120. The ratio is 0.78.

> *But be ye doers of the word, and not hearers only, deceiving your own selves.*
> — *James 1:22 KJV*

America's changing demographics project that there will be twice as many retirees in America in the year 2030, but only 18% more workers. The need to revamp Social Security has been mentioned for the past three presidential administrations. I use the word "mentioned" because nothing has changed beyond discussion. Both Social Security and Medicare are headed for a deficit. Congress and the President will have to come up with an agreeable plan soon. To remedy this, Congress could tax the next generation at much higher rates to pay for the Social Security of their parents; or perhaps increase the retirement eligibility age beyond age 62, or a combination of the two. One thing is certain: Without drastic change, Social Security will not be able to pay the forecasted payments. That's why I urge you to take control of your destiny. Become a doer of the Fire Your Debt spending plan. Walk out the steps in this spending plan and you will eliminate debt. Then, take your previous debt payments and begin saving and investing. Use one of the wealth calculators on our FireYourDebt.com website to determine the future value of your savings and investments. Now you can see a vision more clearly of how this money can grow and provide choices for you and your family.

GET READY TO GRADUATE!

For promotion cometh neither from the east, nor from the west, nor from the south. But God is the judge: He putteth down one, and setteth up another.
— Psalm 75:6-7 KJV

Retirement is a myth to many Americans. They do not believe they will be able to retire. Interestingly, in my studies, I have only discovered one Scripture in which God speaks of retirement. In Numbers 8:25 (NLT), God instructs the priests to retire from the work in the tabernacle at age 50. But in the next verse, He tells them that they can continue with the guard duty of securing the tabernacle of God. God gave us instruction in Genesis 1. He tells us to be *fruitful, multiply* and *replenish* the earth and *SUBDUE* it.

He who gathers money little by little makes it grow.
— Proverbs 13:11 KJV

If God has told us he wants us to be fruitful, multiply and replenish and SUBDUE the world, where do we begin?

I coach many people who want to go straight to the multiplication process. Who wouldn't want to microwave their money into quick millions? However, God has a plan. Most people wouldn't know how to manage a million dollars in one lump sum. But, as they increase little by little, they begin to understand their role as a steward of these larger resources for God. Therefore, we must begin by becoming fruitful. You do this by saving systematically. You have to be fruitful to move to the second step of multiplying. Multiplication happens when you take your savings and begin to invest it. It is God's money. We should be knowledgeable stewards of where we are investing it. That requires a plan and a strategy to always invest in good ground (quality investments). We also need a diversification strategy for our investments that I mentioned in Chapter 6 to begin hiring your wealth.

Give portions to seven, yes to eight, for you do not know what disaster will come upon the land.
— Ecclesiastes 11:2 NIV

We become fruitful when we save money. We multiply through investing in a diversified portfolio with high quality investments. I encourage you to research Index funds. They are a good product to diversify with. Then God tells us to replenish. You replenish by giving. God is more interested in getting money *through* you than *to* you. When you give, you are sowing money. You have now completed the cycle. Save, invest and give. By saving, investing and giving, you stay in a continuous loop of God's favor. He will see your heart and give you more to save, invest and give. After successfully implementing these three steps, God says we should subdue the world. Are you ready to get started?

The priest in Number 8:25 retired from their tabernacle duties, but not from life. They graduated to a new level of service. They began the process of training priestly successors. They became the "one up" mentor to the new priesthood. I believe that retirement is a "graduation" to a different level of life's work and service. The life skills you have accumulated can be used in different ways to fulfill your life's mission. I believe His plans and purposes for us include a period in our lives in which we are able to accomplish this.

> *In all thy ways acknowledge him, and he shall direct thy paths.*
> — *Proverbs 3:6 KJV*

Therefore, the first step in retirement planning is to consult God in your plans. Carla and I developed our retirement plan in 1984. We wanted to create a choice to retire by age 50, which was 2000. By being fruitful, multiplying and replenishing, we were able to accumulate the amount of money we needed to retire by age 46. However, God was the One who gave me favor and promotions at work. That favor put me in position to have options. Since my promotions came from God, I sought clear

> **You have to become fruitful in order to multiply.**

direction from Him. I wanted to be sure that my plans were in sync with His timing. It is one thing to have enough money to walk away; it is another thing to walk away from the plans and purposes God has for you. I had to obtain the peace from God before deciding to leave my company. It was a cool evening in Brazil, while on a business trip, when I received this peace. Upon my return I had a discussion with Compaq's CEO. We developed a four-month transition for me. I left Compaq Computer on March 31, 1999, at age 48. The world calls this retirement. I call it "graduation!" Since my graduation, I have been busy teaching others how to fire debt and hire wealth. My life's mission is to multiply myself to increase the number of God's children into a debt-free, wealth creation position that allows them to graduate to their purpose in life.

REPLACE THE PERIOD WITH A COMMA

Plans fail for lack of counsel, but with many advisors they succeed.
— Proverbs 15:22

The plans of the Lord stand firm forever.
— Psalm 33:11

It is easy to make excuses for not being able to retire. Many people have told me, "I am too old; it is too late to accumulate enough money." Others declare, "Social Security will not be there for me when I qualify for it." Still others have said to me, "Greg, I don't even know how to *read* my 401K statement, let alone understand how well the plan is preparing me for retirement." But as we have learned, excuses will keep you a permanent resident of Debt City. You can overcome your objections with a plan *and* action. When people say they don't believe Social Security will be available when they retire, they put a period at the end of the sentence. If this represents your feelings, I encourage you today to replace the period with a comma. After, the comma, add: "...but I WILL develop a plan that allows me to retire *without* Social Security." With God, you can become the exception to the rule.

This is how to take control of your situation:

Pray and plan.

Because Americans are surrounded by the tokens of wealth, we bind ourselves with debt and spend in excess of our incomes. In 2005, economists reported America had a negative savings rate. Americans spent all of their disposable income; then many dipped into their home equity and took out a loan to finance other purchases. In Mark 13:22, Jesus called this the "deceitfulness of riches." While we look prosperous to other countries, in reality we are in debt up to our eyeballs. Americans certainly have freedom to go into debt. But debt "freedom," unchecked by a vision with goals, leads to financial slavery. Out-of-control spending and debt accumulation leaves consumers enslaved to their jobs. The domino effect is that the majority of Americans are just two or three paychecks away from financial disaster. It is never too late to begin to plan *today.*

THE WINNING SCORE

How much money do you need for retirement? How much is "enough?" Enough is the amount of money you need to fulfill your retirement vision and goals. It's possible to calculate a more concrete dollar amount to this question, but the answer is not a one time only calculation. Originally, some money management gurus placed the retirement "winning score" at around $1 million. With inflation, that prediction has crept upward to $2 million. The true amount of money is different for everybody; there is not a "one size fits all" financial plan. Everybody has a different amount of debt, different levels of savings and incomes, and different vision and goals. With that in mind, I recommend using the 10 % guideline for retirement savings as a starting point. Deduct 10 % of each paycheck and direct it towards your retirement savings. There is no hard and fast rule about 10%. God created you to be unique. Your spending plan and retirement plan is unique to you too.

FIRST THINGS FIRST

One thing is certain: The stock market will go up and it will go down. We always hope it goes up more often than it goes down, but that's not always the case. People who begin investing in the stock market without first calculating their "winning score" often become emotional when they see a few days of market declines. I have seen people become emotionally involved with their investments. When you know your winning score, you will become "emotionally immune" to the volatile stock market.

Calculate your winning score by inflating your current expenses and matching these costs with the compounded growth of your savings and investments. In other words, if your expenses are $3,000 a month today and inflation averages 3% per year, and you wish to retire in 25 years, it will take $6,098 a month in 25 years to buy what $3,000 a month does today. The matching or comparison that occurs next is calculating your forecasted growth of your savings and investments and then deducting your annual inflated cost of living from your investments. While this might sound complicated, seek a retirement web site to provide this information.

Once you can calculate your winning score, you can begin to see clearly what you must do beginning with your next paycheck. In this chapter, you will learn what you need to do to prepare for retirement, no mater what stage in life you are in. The later you begin the larger percentage above 10% you will need to save. You need to be a good steward of your money for God. Always align changes in your plan to your retirement vision and goals. Review your plan every time you receive a raise or a bonus. In the next few sections, I am going to dissect the winning score equation into smaller bites according to different age groups with different incomes, savings and expenses.

THE 30-MINUTE MAKEOVER

Take thirty minutes each month to review your retirement plan. Retirement is not a 'once upon a time' story; it is reality. I encourage you to face it head-on. Make sure your plan can finance your life mission. Nearly 70% of pre-retirees report they plan to work part time or never retire at all. Develop a 20/20 retirement vision. Remember, it is really graduation. Today's retirees do not sit around and do nothing. You are reaching a point in life where you will have choices; a choice to volunteer at your church; a choice to go on mission trips; a choice to spend time with your children or grandchildren. You will have more choices if you begin today to fire debt and hire wealth.

RETIREMENT STRATEGIES

In this section, let's look at various retirement scenarios. Again, I understand that not everyone has already put a retirement strategy in place – even in your fifties. However, it's not too late to have a successful retirement. We'll use five groups of people, at various life stages and "entry points" into their retirement plan. Please bear with me in these different strategies. I will use many numbers that I calculated from a retirement program I wrote. This program comprehends the current spending with inflation and marries it to the compounded growth of the savings and investments to answer the question of the winning score as I addressed above in the first things first section. Consider these models or templates for your plan. This software will be available in the second half of 2006 on www.FireYourDebt.com

GROUP ONE – THE HIGH SCHOOL GRADUATE

This group graduated from high school at age 18. They found jobs after high school and work 44 years until they are 62. They do not go on to college. This first group is at an advantage, since they cannot obtain credit cards until they are 18.They are the easiest group to calculate the realization of a million dollars. They have four more income-generating years than college graduates from Group 2. If they are taught to be the lenders and not the borrowers, they also will be blessed with four more years of compound growth. Statistics tell us they will not make the higher lifetime earnings of the college graduate, yet they can become millionaires and retire comfortable if they stay focused.

Each person in this category needs to know that they can and will need to become a millionaire to retire comfortably. If you are in your 30's or younger, you will probably need more than $1 million at retirement time. However, this will be calculated based upon your vision, goals and spending. Realistically, the more a person makes, the more they spend. Continuing with this calculation over a 40 plus year working life, determines the amount of millions Group One will need. Today, approximately 8.5 million people in America are millionaires, representing slightly less than 3% of Americans. Group One needs to begin thinking and acting like millionaires today.

If Group One begins work at age 18, making $7 an hour and receives an average 4% per year pay increase while experiencing a 3% inflation rate, in effect, they are 1% ahead of inflation per year. If they begin with the 10/10/80 rule mentioned earlier in this chapter, they save 70 cents an hour the first year of employment. Since they are 18, they can begin to be more aggressive in their investments. At this age, they should be 100% in stocks. Index funds would probably be a good investment vehicle to be in stocks while simultaneously being diversified.

If this first group saves 70 cents per hour, working 2000 hours per year, after the first year they have saved $1400. As they receive their 4% raises each year, we plan their savings will increase 4% as well. I have calculated a 12% return on their investments since they are 100% in stocks. Later in life, they should use the Monte Carlo simulation to better factor a forecasted annual return on their investments. They would achieve $1 million at age 53. Notice here that after they focus on their savings and vision, the longest period of wealth accumulation is the first million dollars. Using the rule of 72, which is the doubling rule, it states that the interest you receive divided into 72 will be the length of time for your money to double. This occurs without adding any new money. Therefore, the doubling occurs sooner since Group One is saving 10% (including all the raises.) Group One continues to work past age 53 and continues to save 10% and invest in stocks at a 12% forecasted growth. They reach the second million dollar goal only six years later, by age 59. They reach over three million dollars three years later, at age 62. In summary, Group One worked 35 years and realized $1 million in savings, in 41 years they realized $2 million in savings and in 44 years they realized $3.1 million in savings.

Here is an amazing parallel for you to consider. At age 62, Group One has saved and invested for 44 years. They now have a $3.1 million retirement account. Remember, they began working at age 18 at $7 an hour and received 4% salary increases per year. In the 44 years of working, their total lifetime earnings are $1.7 million. In other words, their retirement account is *176% more* than their total gross pay after working for 44 years.

But is $3.1 million dollars enough for Group One at 3% inflation? At age 62, their annual salary is $78,631 based upon 4% average wage increases. If they retire at age 62, they only need to replace 80% of their income since they had 10% allocated to tithe and 10% to savings. This calculates their living expenses to be $62,905 a year. At retirement, they would not want to be invested 100% in stocks but move to a more conservative investment allocation. Assuming they realized a 7% return and were in the 25% tax bracket, in the first year of retirement, after taxes, their retirement account would earn over $162,000 while they spent $62,905. Therefore, $99,000 was added to their retirement account at age 63 to continue working for them.

Remember, the tithe was removed from the living expense calculation since Group One receives income from their retirement account. We also planned the retirement account would grow 7% per year. The tithe is on all your increase. Therefore at an increase of $162,000, tithe would be paid at $16,200, thus leaving our increase at $99,000 less $16,200= $82,800.

The 10/10/80 plan will work for Group One if they implement and achieve the assumptions for savings at 10% and investment growth at 12%. This doesn't happen automatically. It requires Group One to increase their abilities and get a mentor to teach them how to invest. The 12% was a planning number. Ideally, as Group One ages, they begin to change their asset allocation to be more conservative than 100% stocks.

GROUP TWO – THE COLLEGE GRADUATE

This group graduated from college and began a career at about age 22. This category represents ages 22-29. While Group One enters their earning years without debt, the average Group Two person enters with student loan debt that is 85 percent higher among four-year public university college graduates from a decade ago. Recent graduates owed an average of $15,100 in 1999/2000, up from $8,200 in 1989/1990. Student loan debt increased by 55 percent among recent graduates of private four-year colleges with student loan debt. These graduates owed an average of $16,500 in 1999/2000, compared to $10,600 in 1989/1990 (all figures in 2002 dollars).

In 2000, Nellie Mae, a prominent lender of educational loans, examined credit card ownership among undergraduate and graduate students who were applying for credit-based loans with Nellie Mae. Their survey found that 78% of undergraduates (aged 18-25) have at least one credit card. Ninety-five percent of the graduate students surveyed had at least one card. Undergraduates carried an average balance of $2,748 while graduate students carried an average balance of $4,776. Nellie Mae also found that of the 78% of undergraduates with a card; 32% have four or more cards; 13% have credit card debt between $3,000 and $7,000; and 9% have credit card debt greater than $7,000 (Nellie Mae, 2000).

High school graduates earn an average of $1.2 million over their working life. Associate's degree holders earn about $1.6 million; and bachelor's degree holders earn about $2.1 million. Using the lifetime earnings of $2.1 million and the same 4% increases working 40 years until they are 62, and using the 10/10/80 rule; plus a forecasted return on investment of 12%, the college graduate begins their career making $21,500 per year. After 40 years they also have $3 million in their retirement account. Even though they made $500,000 more in lifetime earnings than the high school graduate, the high school graduate in Group One actually has almost $100,000 more in retirement savings than the college graduate. Why? Four more years of compounding growth of working.

Is $3 million retirement savings enough for Group Two? The answer is yes, IF they didn't fall into the following categories of college graduate debt. At age 62, their annual income with the 4% annual salary increases is $103,222. They need to replace 80% of this salary in retirement calculating an annual need of $82,578. Their retirement income also is moved to a conservative 7% portfolio and they are in a 25% tax bracket. Therefore, they earn $157,000 after taxes and spend $82,578. They pay their tithe on the increase, as did Group One.

> *Make your vision of financial victory crystal-clear.*

Comprehending these two types of debt, the average Group Two people enter work life with a debt load of approximately $20,000 plus a possible automobile loan. If a Group Two person does not have a vision or life goals, they may find themselves coming home to live with their parents until they pay down their student loan debts.

If you are a parent of a Group One or Two young adult, one of the greatest financial gifts you can give him or her is an education on how to manage and invest money. You can have a positive influence on their financial future by sharing this information. It can also be very advantageous to your finances as your young adult becomes financially independent.

Group One and Group Two each have an important ally: time. Couple time with a passion to fire debt, and each group will be able retire comfortably and independently of Social Security. Note, the above calculations are also based upon individual retirement savings and would improve greatly in a company 401K plan where most have a company match of a percentage of your savings.

These are scenarios to challenge you to figure your retirement answer. Your level of risk determines your projected investment strategy. As you become more educated in investing, you should begin to think long term about the taxes that will be due upon withdrawals and develop a strategy to pay the minimum taxes.

Spending money is a natural process; saving is unnatural. It's a character attribute that must be taught. I believe most people in Groups One and Two do not know how to save; therefore it is also unlikely they know how to invest. These two groups have assumptions in the calculations. I encourage you to prepare your plan and learn how to achieve the assumptions you plan for. A retirement plan crystallizes your vision of financial victory. It will paint you a financial target. The bull's-eye represents the winning score.

GROUP THREE – THE GROWING FAMILY

This category represents people in their 30's. Most Group Three people are still paying off their student loans. In addition, they probably have increased their credit card debt, added a mortgage, and began a family. Group Three represents the first generation to grow up with the Internet. They have been marketed to and live with more peer pressure than any previous generation. Without parents to teach them about money and investing, this group has an immature attitude towards money. Group Three could be the most indebted generation in modern history. As a result, Group Three may be the first generation still paying for pizza they ate 10 years before while in college!

They are also the first group that aspires to live the same lifestyle or better than their parents today. However, they don't comprehend what took their parents a lifetime to accumulate cannot be accomplished in a few years. Group Three is on a path to become the first generation ever, in America, not to achieve a higher standard of living than their parents; because of debt. Consequently, Group Three has become the first group with a "minimum monthly payment" mentality. Group Three thinks their student loan isn't too bad. It's just a bill. After all, only $100 a month for a $20,000 student loan and the interest rate is only 4.25%. Wake up! At that rate, it will take *29 years* to pay off that student loan. The cumulative interest is $14,851.

Obviously, a 30-yr.old has nine more years to use time as their ally than the person who is 39. My intention in grouping ages is to allow you a section that you can refer to in each stage of your life. Since credit was easy to obtain in college, it became easier to increase post graduation. Without a vision, spending plan and discipline, Group Three represents a generation that is skating on thin financial ice.

What can Group Three do? Begin by estimating a retirement nest egg amount you desire to accumulate. For this example, we will assume $2 million. A rule of thumb to apply is not to withdraw more than 4% of your retirement account per year. This means you would need to plan to live on $80,000 a year plus any Social Security benefits. Take a 35-yr.old Group Three person who earns $40,000 a year net and plans to work until age 65. A 3% inflation rate means that he or she will need $94,263 at age 65 to equal the same purchasing power of $40,000 at age 35. Therefore, Social Security would need to supply the $14,263 shortage. In this scenario, Group Three has to allow the federal government to control part of their retirement security. If they withdrew 6% per year, they would be independent of the need of Social Security. However, the $2,000,000 would be depleted in less than 20 years. The more logical choice is to increase the savings above the 10% level to build a retirement account of $2.4 million. This eliminates the need for Social Security. Since they know their winning score is $2.4 million, Group Three can easily accomplish their goals. Time is their ally.

Group Three should apply the Fire Your Debt spending plan and be aggressive at firing debt. They should fire the student loan as fast as they can with their 4% pay raises. Since they have less time to fund retirement than Group One and Two, this group needs more than the 10% savings. Once all debt is fired, the previous debt payments must go to savings.

Salary increase must apply the rules you implemented in your strategy for increase. Always tithe first on your increase and apply the remaining 90% to your goals. Group Three will be successful if they stay focused on their winning retirement score.

What about the person who is 39 years old and at the end of the Group Three range? If they plan to retire of age 65, they have 26 working years remaining. Can they retire at their winning score if they have 0$ saved today? The answer is also yes – but it is more difficult. If they earn $44,000 net a year today at 3% inflation, they will need $92,000 a year in 26 years. At 4% withdrawals at age 65, they need a winning score of $2.3 million. They have 26 years to save and invest to accomplish this. It is possible but more difficult than with Group One or Two.

GROUP FOUR – BABY BOOMERS & BABY BUSTERS

Group Four are the people in their 40's. This is the mid-career group. They have been out of school for about 20 to 25 years; they have 20 to 25 years remaining to work. Group Four should follow the plans for Group Three. After all debt is fired, the previous debt payments must go to savings. Salary increase must apply the rules you implemented in your strategy for increase. Always tithe first on your increase and apply the remaining 90% to your goals. However, Group Four has less time than Group Three and needs to be more conservative in their investment risks. Mid-career people should begin the asset reallocation process to ensure more safety of principle and less risk of a total stock portfolio. Group Four should think about cutting risk by adding some bonds. Group Four should be in or approaching peak earnings in these years. They should add to their retirement fund every time they pay off a debt or get a salary increase. They should contribute the maximum their 401K plan allows each year and also fund a Roth IRA each year.

Determining the lump sum dollar amount you need to support a comfortable retirement lifestyle is a difficult part of the financial equation. Group Four has fewer years to save for retirement. If they reallocate their savings to include bonds, they could likely see an 8% return on their investment. Each person needs to determine their own risk reward ratio. Most Group Four people have not yet saved the lump retirement sum that they need. One way to increase your retirement account is to employ the home payoff accelerator in your retirement strategy. To use this strategy effectively, first decide that as soon as you pay off your mortgage, that principle and interest now goes into retirement savings. When I forecast a scenario for people using this strategy, they are surprised how much they can accumulate late in life. Without a plan, most people would consider buying another home late in life with a 30-year mortgage. Most haven't thought about the mortgage extending into their retirement years.

A few years ago, I met with a couple, age 58, which had a 30 year mortgage. They were self employed and planned to work all their lives and pay off the mortgage at age 88. As I reviewed their financial assets, I discovered a whole life insurance policy that had significant cash value in it. When they began their business they were required to take out this policy for $1 million face value. The cash value had grown to over $150,000. My suggestion to them was to determine now what life insurance they needed. Next, purchase this amount in a 20-year level term life insurance policy. After they were accepted for this policy, then cash in the whole life policy and pay off the mortgage. A few months after we met, they invited Carla and me over for dinner. After dinner, they brought out matches and the mortgage and we all participated in burning the mortgage. They became debt-free. Now, they are focused on hiring wealth. After they paid off the mortgage and no longer had to pay for a whole life insurance policy, they now had more than $2,000 per month to invest for retirement. While this couple's age fits Group Five, which we discuss later, this example of paying the mortgage off and moving that money to the retirement savings fits for all homeowners or those who plan to purchase a home for the first time.

Americans have become very mobile. Low interest rates allow us to refinance our mortgages; some several times. Buying a home and committing to a 30-year mortgage is a tradition that causes most people to never consider actually owning a home. My strategy for home ownership is twofold: 1) only get a 15-year mortgage; 2) do not allow your monthly payment to be more than 25% of your gross monthly pay. Then as you pay off other debts and receive raises, your strategy for increase allows the home to be paid off much earlier than 15 years. Now, you are debt-free and all the principle, interest and additional principle can be applied to saving and investing.

Unfortunately, the average American sells their home seven years into a 30-year mortgage. They buy a more expensive home and begin the 30-year mortgage all over again. If they did this four times in their working life, they would have a 51-year mortgage (three homes at seven years each and the fourth at 30 years). Let's do the mortgage company's math. Say, you have a 6.5% mortgage and move in seven years. Your original loan was $135,000, which results in a principle and interest payment of $853.29 a month. After seven years, you paid $71,676.36 but you still owe $122,062. In other words, you reduced the mortgage $12,938 but paid $71,676 resulting in 553% simple interest, but it is called a 6.5% loan. Sounds like fuzzy math; but in reality, your mortgage payment interest is calculated each month on the loan balance. Therefore, the interest is front-loaded on your monthly payments. Buying the right home for the long term and staying put will be a reason Group Four will be able to retire successfully. Learn about amortization schedules before you ever take out a mortgage. A 6.5% loan on $150,000 mortgage for 30 years results in interest of $191,316. It doesn't look like 6.5% but it is according to amortization schedules of interest rates.

It is not too late for Group Four even if they do not have any money saved. A 45-year old wanting to work 20 more years who is making $50,000 a year today will need $87,765 a year at age 65 to have the same purchasing power at a 3% inflation rate. If they get debt-free and were saving at retirement, they probably need to generate 80% of the $87,765 or they would need to plan to have $5,851 per month. If Social Security paid $1,851 a month, a Group Four person needs all other incomes to produce $4,000 a month. Using the rule of thumb to not withdraw more than 4% of your retirement nest egg, this 45 year old person needs a nest egg of $1,200,000. 4% withdrawals equal $48,000 a year or 4%.

How could they accumulate $1,200,000 in 20 years? Everyone's plans are unique so we need to make some assumptions. They have no savings today. Their company matches in a 401K plan fifty cents on the dollar up to 6%. They become debt-free, except for the mortgage in 5 years. Previous debts were $1,500 per month. Their mortgage has 10 years remaining and the principle and interest is $1,225 per month. At age 50, they begin saving $1,500 per month plus the company match adds $125 per month. At 8% return they have $123,551 at the end of five years. Now the mortgage is paid off and they save the principle and interest for the next 10 years until age 65. At age 65, they have $801,812. Not enough for their goal of $1,200,000 yet. It would take another four years of work, until age 69 to reach $1,200,000. The good news is we did not apply a strategy for increase. With salary increases and possible bonuses the strategy would be to tithe first and use the remaining 90% to begin retirement savings earlier.

This is just an example. There are many Web sites, including ours, that help you to calculate your financial winning score. In order to take control, you need to know this number. While it will not be a perfect number, it establishes a goal for you to accomplish. Group Four can begin in mid-career to retire successfully but absolutely must be aggressive in firing debt and hiring wealth.

GROUP FIVE –FACING THE FUTURE

Group Five are the group who are over 50. What can you do if your numbers do not add up? Perhaps you are in this group. If you have not put a retirement plan in place other than expecting Social Security to take up the slack, you may feel as if you are on a high-wire without a safety net. Unfortunately, for more than half of soon to be retiree's Social Security represents over half of their income sources. We are not in the 'Once upon a time' years in America, when people reached age 65, retired in a home that was paid for, drove a new car they paid cash for, received a pension and Social Security that paid all their expenses and had company-provided health insurance. My grandparents lived in that age. That is not the case any longer; you must take responsibility for your needs in retirement. Remember there is hope. First of all, Group Five must be very aggressive at firing debt and reducing consumption; then aggressively hire wealth.

There is some good news: Social Security will be there for Group Five. However, it will only take care of 30% to 45% of their expenses. Save and invest in conservative investment choices. Group Five must stick with the safety of financial principal and aggressively accumulate cash; the risk of aggressive stock investments for most of them will be too great. Data between 1991 and 2005 from the Principal Financial Group for the return on investment for large cap growth companies returned an average 9.89%, core bonds returned 7.28% and high yield bonds returned 10.39%. Allocating a third to each of these asset classes would produce a forecasted return annually of 9.18%. I am just calculating a simple scenario to provide somewhat of a conservative planning approach to investing late in life. This scenario results in less risk than Group One or Two can risk. For Group Five, they need investment returns that are less risky.

A spending plan for Group Five is a great benefit. It helps create a process for them to manage every dollar and live within their means. In all likelihood, a person in their 50's has some level of retirement savings. As they approach retirement, perhaps a reallocation to more core bonds and away from Large cap growth stocks will be in order to protect principle. All of these types of investments would be great places to begin to educate you in financial matters.

Every available dollar needs to be working for this group. If a Group Five person has not paid their home off and directed these funds to retirement savings, this is their first priority. If you are 50 and make $3,000 per month net today, you will need $4,500 per month at age 65. If Social Security pays $1,500 per month, you need investment income of $3,000 per month at age 65. However, if you paid your final mortgage payment at age 55, and reduced your expenses by $900 per month, your monthly expenses after Social Security at age 65 will need to be $1,800 instead of $3,000. This means you need a retirement nest egg of approximately $500,000 at age 65.

If they apply all of the previous debt payments to investing, actively pursue the spending plan and fire debt within five years, Group Five should be able to retire without regrets. There is no need for you to make sacrifices in your retirement years if you begin *today* to fire debt and hire wealth. By taking control of your finances today, you become the author of your autobiography. Your story will be one of success and prosperity because you implemented God's plan for you. You became the lender and not the borrower.

SIX STEPS TO A SECURE RETIREMENT

Let's begin with our foundation. Here are six steps to set in place for a successful retirement. Carla and I developed these steps in 1984 and have lived our lives according to these steps ever since. Note: The key to this success is to be in financial covenant with God. You must continually perform steps 1 and 2 according to Malachi 3.

    1. **Tithe on your income.** There is no statute of limitations on God's commandment to tithe. The good news is that you don't *have* to tithe; you *get* to tithe, so that even in retirement, God is still blessing you. It is a way to show God that you are placing your trust in Him by giving him back the first tenth of all of your increase. Most people never consider the rest of the tithe. There

is more than tithing from each paycheck. The more I am referring to is your retirement savings. For example, if you are tithing today on your gross income and saving in your company's 401K plan; your 401K plan has three components: 1) The money you saved; 2) the company match; and 3) the multiplication of the investments. You have already tithed on the money you saved. Recognize there is a tithe due on the money matched by your company *and* the investment growth. In the mid 1990's, Carla and I experienced a financial breakthrough. I calculated these three numbers and tithed on all the paper profits from all my investments. During the last three years I worked, our net worth tripled. I contribute this increase to tithing to God on all the increase even though we had not physically taken possession of the increase. We continue to tithe annually on all our paper profits. Paper profits are the realization of the increase in our investments even though we have not sold them. In effect, we are giving to God the increase now, and not waiting for these to be paid when we die and our estate is settled. Tithing builds your solid foundation for the financial house you are building.

2. **Commit to give offerings above the tithe.** Tithing, step one, is paying to God what is His. The offering, step two, is given, not paid. It is over and above the tithe. Psalm 35:27 says that God has pleasure in the prosperity of His children. When you plan for steps one and two, you are preparing to open the windows of Heaven over your finances. God doesn't give us a specific amount to give. However, He does tell us in 2 Corinthians 9:6 that the amount we give determines the amount we get back. You can not out-give God. Be sure to include an offering in your spending plan and expect God to increase back to you. A metaphor to think how this works is "the hole you give through is the hole you receive through."

3. **Include a detailed strategy for firing ALL debt before you retire.** "All debts" includes your primary home. More than 90% of the spending plans I've created for people result in them firing all their debts, except their mortgage, within five years. Entering retirement totally debt-free means you will have choices because all of your expenses will be variable (controllable) expenses.

4. **You must continue to save.** Not only save but the retirement model of the new millennium is all about saving more. As you pay off debts, the temptation will be to use the money to buy other things. I encourage you to wait to buy things after you are well on the path to a successful retirement. Save or invest the money you paid on your debts. Another option is to use the surplus as additional principle, pay off your mortgage faster, and then take all this previous debt money and save and invest it.

5. **You must plan for inflation.** Inflation has been at 4.1% for the past 50 years in America. 4.1% doesn't sound like much until you analyze it over time. If you spend $3,000 a month in 2006, at 4.1% average annual inflation, you will need $6,701 in 2026 to have the same purchasing power that $3,000 does today. Inflation will occur. We must plan for it to be successful.

6. **You must plan for taxes.** If your primary source of retirement savings is in your 401K plan, there will be taxes due when you begin taking distributions from your 401K plan. No one can calculate the tax rate at the moment, but be aware that your tax rate when you begin withdrawing money could be higher than it is today. This is because of the previous mentioned federal deficits and shortages in Social Security and Medicare. Planning for tithe and taxes is a must for a successful retirement plan.

Everyone needs to buy retirement. It is a major purchase that few think about early in life. But the younger the person, the less they need to save weekly to buy retirement. I encourage you to plan *today* to build your retirement wealth account. God said in His covenant promise that He gave us the abilities to produce wealth. Use your abilities, beginning with your next paycheck to hire wealth.

In Chapter 8, I will teach you the process of "Becoming a Financial Leader." Each of us, no matter where we start in life, with the right attitude and tools in our toolkit, has the capacity to lead ourselves from Debt City into abundance. You'll learn how to develop your financial team, sharpen your vision, and attack the "Goliaths" that threaten your financial success.

EXPECTATIONS

1. I will develop a retirement strategy that allows me to retire without Social Security.
2. By saving, investing and giving, I will stay in a continuous loop of God's favor.
3. I will stay focused on my winning retirement score.
4. When I do "graduate" (retire) I will use my abilities to teach others.
5. By taking control of my finances today, I will become the author of my own successful autobiography.

8

BECOMING A
FINANCIAL CHAMPION

The God of heaven will prosper us.
— Nehemiah 2:20 NIV

The book of Nehemiah is an excellent book on leadership. Nehemiah, the king's cupbearer, had a good job, access to the King, and a comfortable lifestyle, but word comes to him that the walls of Jerusalem are still torn down. Although he had never even seen Jerusalem, his spirit was moved. As you read, you learn that Nehemiah did something he was not qualified to do. He never received training for the task of rebuilding the walls. He just did it! Not only did Nehemiah come up with the plan, he also got others to believe in their own abilities to rebuild the walls. Many historians read this book and think it is inaccurate. It seems impossible to totally restore the walls of Jerusalem in only 52 days. It happened; all because one man got a vision, created a plan, pursued it with passion and got others to become passionate too.

> *Be a real champion. Go to God for your battle plan.*

YOU ARE A CHAMPION

A city without walls is defenseless. Nehemiah knew this. That's why he stepped forward to rebuild the walls of Jerusalem. A family without a financial plan is defenseless. Defeated debt allows you to use your abilities to build your wall. You can be a financial champion. Financial champions step forward to solve their wealth creation problem. You have the victory. Jesus said on the cross, "It is finished." A champion sees beyond the dangers and risks. A champion sees the walls standing even though today they lie as rubble. Champions may be initially surrounded by debt, but they rebuild their financial house. Every time they save and invest, they, like Nehemiah, are rebuilding their financial fortress. Nehemiah prayed four months for a task that took less than two months to complete. A champion goes to God for the battle plan, and then gives God the glory when the battle is won. After restoration, Nehemiah sealed the victory with order. He gave orders how to take care of God's house and the city. All of them knew what their role was.

Modern society is so preoccupied with celebrities and popularity contests that most would not recognize a true champion if they met one. At the time of this writing, the 2006 Winter Olympics has just ended. Millions of viewers around the world watched and predicted the event outcome; some even complained that their favorite didn't win. None of the "armchair athletes" were competing. Most of the *real* athletes had been training since childhood for their one opportunity at Olympic greatness. They were willing to train a lifetime even though their event might last less than a minute. Becoming a financial champion may not take a lifetime – but it does take a cause. Is being in Debt City a big enough cause for you to become a financial champion?

Are you willing to go the extra mile and do something about your financial picture? Are you willing to expand your prayer time, establish a vision with supportable goals, and *declare war on debt?* Today is the day to birth the financial champion. Today is your day of victory. You can do more in a moment of prayer with God than you can do in a lifetime without Him. God doesn't create mistakes. It doesn't matter where you have been. It is where you are going that will determine your success. If Nehemiah could accomplish this great task, so can you. After all, God says this to be true in Acts 10:34 by declaring He is not a respecter of people. If He did this for Nehemiah, He will do it for you.

THE PACKAGE IS NOT THE GIFT

God uses people because of their character, integrity and morals; not their stature. King Saul was the first king of Israel. He was tall and good looking. Even today, people look to outward appearance as they seek a hero to follow. Compare Saul to Nehemiah. Nehemiah was an ordinary man with extraordinary talent. He had a zeal for God. He set high standards; this caused others to adapt to those standards. Nehemiah took four months in chapter 1 to pray in order to get a clear business plan in place. He caught the vision! Then, because he displayed leadership qualities, he was able to get others to catch the vision.

DO YOU KNOW WHO YOU ARE?

There are many Biblical leaders who didn't know they were leaders until God communicated it to them. While Moses was tending sheep in Midian, God gave him his new assignment. He was to go back to Egypt and deliver God's children from the tyranny of Pharaoh. Moses' reply to God was, 'Who, me?' What will be your response at your own burning bush? Sometimes a leader emerges from within a person confronted with a crisis. We've read about people who rush into burning buildings to rescue strangers or people who pull injured people from an auto collision. A minute before the crisis, they might have said, "Who, me?" Recognize in a split second, a champion sprang forth from them. Because there was both a need, and a situation to fill that need, the person changed from being ordinary to extraordinary. A financial champion gets a vision for change and leads the change.

God asked Moses what was in his hand. Moses replied, "My shepherd's staff." The staff represented Moses' profession. God asked him for it. Immediately this shepherd's staff was transformed into a miracle tool. Moses and Aaron used it many times. Understand what occurred when Moses gave God his staff. In effect he was trusting God with the implement of his profession. A successful leader will put their job into God's hands.

GOD CREATED YOU FOR A TIME LIKE THIS

An angel of God approached Gideon in Judges 6. The angel's salutation to Gideon was, "(you) mighty man of God." Look at Gideon's response: "First, if I am a mighty man of God, why has all this evil fallen on us? Where are all the miracles our fathers told us about and now God has forsaken us and delivered us into the hands of the enemy?" (Judges 6:13 KJV) The angel used the same process God used with Moses. He threw the situation right back at Gideon. Gideon wanted to host a pity party. He wanted sympathy, but God was looking for a leader. God saw what was inside of Gideon. The angel then told Gideon to get up and go in his might and save Israel from the enemy. Once again, Gideon made an excuse: "How can I do this, my family is poor and I am the least in my father's house?" Judges 6:15 KJV. Gideon not only made excuses for his inaction, but he also linked his inabilities with his financial situation. He *declared himself* the least in his father's house. Are you like Gideon? Have you thought you could never become a leader because of your current financial situation? God is saying the same thing to you He said to Gideon: "Get up and I will be with you." Judges 6:16 KJV

> *You can rebuild your walls to keep debt out forever.*

And Jesus looking upon them saith, With men it is impossible...
— *Mark 10:27 KJV*

Skeptics told Nehemiah the task of rebuilding the walls was impossible, but Nehemiah didn't listen to them. Nehemiah's enemies laughed at him. Here Nehemiah was, standing in Jerusalem, a city he had never seen before, looking at a city with torn-down walls and the enemy ridiculing him nearby. Nehemiah was a person of destiny and purpose. So are you. If you are frustrated today about your financial situation, do as Nehemiah did. Begin with a change of perspective. With God's help, you can create wealth. You can retire without regrets. You can rebuild your walls to *keep debt out forever*.

PASSION & PURPOSE

Position and title are not important to God. He created you with purpose and destiny. Today, you can do as Moses, Gideon or Nehemiah did. None of them had bachelor's degrees in leadership. None of them were qualified by external standards. However, with passion and faith in God, they performed miracles. It is time to become passionate about the debt that is limiting your potential. There is a financial leader in you. All you have to do is move. As you move, God will move. All the great leaders in the Bible and today are what we call movers and shakers. Are you ready to become one?

Purpose equals desire plus energy. "For I know the plans I have for you," declares the LORD, plans to prosper you and not to harm you, plans to give you hope and a future. Then you will call upon me and come and pray to me, and I will listen to you. Jeremiah 29:11-12 NIV.

By now you know it is my desire to instill a desire to fire debt and hire wealth in YOU. Now add the energy to your desire like Nehemiah did. If you still feel inadequate, personalize the following verse. God wrote it with you in mind: "Notice among yourselves, dear brothers, that few of you who follow Christ have big names or power or wealth. Instead, God has deliberately chosen to use ideas the world considers foolish and of little worth in order to shame those people considered by the world as wise and great." 1st Corinthians 1:26-27 TLB

> *A righteous man may have many troubles, but the LORD delivers him*
> *from them all.*
> *— Psalm 34:19 NIV*

A limit is a self-imposed boundary. Limited thinking will keep you from rebuilding your financial walls. My pastor, Joel Osteen, always begins our church services by asking the congregation to hold up their Bibles and say in unison, "This is my Bible, I am what the Bible says I am, I can do what the Bible says I can do, I have what the Bible says I have…" This weekly declaration removes limited thinking. It becomes an invitation for the promises of God to manifest in your life. Reciting the affirmation won't make the promises jump out of the Bible into you, but it will require you to use your energy to pursue God's promises.

DEVELOPING YOUR ALL-STAR FINANCIAL TEAM

> *And Jesus looking upon them saith, With men it is impossible, but not with God:*
> *for with God all things are possible.*
> *— Mark 10:27 KJV*

When Nehemiah arrived in Jerusalem, he didn't tell anyone his plans. For three consecutive nights, he went out at night to survey the ruins and develop a strategy. He created an All-Star Team and then energized the people. In 52 days, his team rebuilt the walls of Jerusalem and restored the city's defenses. Some of the stones used to rebuild the walls are the size of rail box cars! The impossible is possible with God. Nehemiah wasn't a promoter, he was a champion. He wasn't a publicist, he was a problem solver. He didn't sit back and say Someone ought to do something about that.

All professional sports leagues have an annual All-Star team. We recognize the people are the best at their position. It is time you begin to create your All-Star team. Nehemiah couldn't rebuild the walls by himself. He needed a team. My All-Star team consists of a trusted CPA who prepares my taxes and offers me advice. It includes a financial planner, who makes recommendations of investments and asset allocation. It includes my wife, Carla, who is in agreement with me. In turn, I am in agreement with her. It includes people who have captured the vision of helping others rebuild their financial walls. It includes mentors that I learn from and gain valuable advice from. It includes my pastor, who teaches me and edifies me with God's Word. It includes a couple of great friends who teach with me and are of like mind. It includes my children, whom I continually teach so they can become mentors to others. I am not an expert in all the areas of finances – but I have access to All-Stars who are.

God gives us great examples of mentoring relationships, such as Elijah and Elisha or Naomi and Ruth. Let me encourage you again to use the "one up and one down" approach to mentorship. Find a good mentor who is successful at what you want to accomplish. As you learn, strive to become qualified to become a mentor in the future.

FACE YOUR FEARS WITH FAITH

A lady who became passionate about becoming the leader over her debt situation wrote this testimonial:

> After setting up a spending and retirement plan, there were a few failures as I tried to stay on this budget. I was determined to change my life and my thinking. The one Scripture I kept quoting was 'a righteous man falls seven times and rises again.' I have enough faith to know if I step out, God will honor my effort. You put me on the envelope method and set up an emergency fund. All of this built (up) my confidence – not only in me, but trusting and watching God work in my life. Each month, my bills are paid. There are no surprises. When

something does come up, I have money in the bank (to cover the expense). What a relief, this is a great way to live—with PEACE. This actually changed other areas of my life as well.

Trusting God is the best way to live. This lady moved from being a slave to her debt to becoming a financial leader.

> *Then he asked me, "Son of man, can these bones become living*
> *people again?"*
> *"O Sovereign LORD," I replied, "you alone know the answer to that."*
> *— Ezekiel 37:3 NLT*

ANSWERING A QUESTION CREATES A SOLUTION

Some people are experts at talking about a problem. Fewer people are experts at solving problems. In late 2005, I went to Guatemala. I was received at the airport by a small group of people, all in their thirties. This group was led by a man who was a fairly new Christian. Shortly after he became a Christian, he started a weekly Bible study at his home. Each week, they discussed current events and problems in their country. Until one day they realized all they discussed were problems. One day, they became fed up with living in an impoverished country. They agreed to no longer discuss a problem without also considering a solution. As a result, they created a group called Guatemala Prospera. They developed a list of what needed to be fixed. Their new vision was to train company executives in leadership principles. I was invited to help train the leaders of the largest bank in Guatemala. I witnessed the

> *If you only talk about your financial problems, nothing changes.*

respect the president of the bank had for Guatemala Prospera. Now, Guatemala Prospera is tackling the idea of re-inventing the education system. These movers and shakers are making a difference.

If you only *talk* about your financial problems, nothing changes. You can't delegate to a mentor to fix your financial problems. You can be a convert and become a problem solver. What is holding you back?

A FEARFUL KING, A FAITHFUL KING

In Revelation 1:6, God has called us kings and priests. He could have used any term, but He specifically used "kings and priests." This is how God sees you! It is time you see yourself the way God sees *you*. God gave us the Old Testament as types and shadows for the New Testament. In the two books of Kings, 42 kings are listed. Each king had a relationship with a priest. The priests were from the tribe of Levi, and the kings were from the 12 tribes of Israel. As we begin reading 1 Kings, God is the King and Samuel the priest. The people complain to Samuel they wanted a man to be their king. God told Samuel He would give them a king, but warned there would be extreme negative results. The people told Samuel they would live with the outcome of their decision. They would rather live in mediocrity than have God remain as their king. They needed a king they could see each day. Kings rule by edict. They establish the government and the laws. A ruler is a highly desirable position and a prestigious position. King Saul became the first king. However, on coronation day, Saul could not be found because he was hiding in fear. He had the same feeling as Moses and Gideon had – "who me?" What was the difference? Moses and Gideon got up and became leaders. Saul hid.

FACING YOUR GOLIATHS IN FAITH

In order to become a king, you have to slay your Goliaths. John Maxwell said a leadership position doesn't give someone courage—but courage can give someone a leadership position. Don't approach your Goliaths looking at your inabilities but rather at your abilities. Billy Graham said courage is contagious; when a brave man takes a stand, the spines of others stiffen.

King Saul eventually led Israel into battle against the Philistines. We are now introduced to Goliath. For 40 days, Goliath came out in the morning and evening; verbally transferring fear into Saul and all his army. Fear is contagious. Courage is also contagious. If God has called you to be a king, you need to become courageous. A young boy named David arrives at the camp of Saul to bring his brothers food. He sees this giant taunting God's army and something happens. In a moment David established his legacy. He became a courageous leader.

PREPARATION PRECEDES PROMOTION

David made a name for himself by facing Goliath, but he became a leader while tending sheep. He had to be self-motivated. He had to use his time wisely. He could have been a lazy person moving only when the sheep moved, but he was out there killing lions and bears in preparation for the battle with Goliath. If you back away from the lion and bear, you will never stand up to your Goliath. When David heard Goliath's taunts, he declared, "Is there not a cause?" Immediately his brothers were all over him. Who do you think you are, they taunted; you are just a kid. Even Saul told David he could not fight the giant. David was at the fork in the road. The fork in the road is a decision point. You are at the fork in the road also. One path is the continuation of what you have been doing; the other path leads to transformation. David could have heeded his brothers' criticism; or conformed to King Saul's fleshly suggestions. Instead, as the Bible said later in 1 Kings 30:6, he "encouraged himself in the Lord." How do you encourage yourself in the Lord? David reminded Saul of his past victories when he killed the lion and the bear.

> *Integrity is doing an excellent job, even when no one sees your work.*

What you realize about David is that he was prepared and confident. Anyone running *towards* a nine-foot giant has to have confidence. His preparation came while he was out in the fields tending sheep. He had to have practiced so much with that slingshot that he knew Goliath was too big to miss. He also knew there was only one place on Goliath that wasn't covered with armor, his forehead. David had become so proficient at the accuracy of his slingshot that he knew he could hit the forehead. No one told David that he should use his spare time practicing with his slingshot while the sheep grazed or slept, but he did. A leader walks in integrity. Integrity is doing an excellent job, even when no one is there to see you working.

Goliath was easy to recognize. He was a giant in full armor protection. David was also easy to recognize. He was the teenager with a sling shot in his hand. Can you imagine how Las Vegas would have handicapped this fight? What hope does David have? Read carefully and see the readiness level of Goliath and David. Goliath was sitting down and wasn't prepared for battle. He spoke some powerful words but David knew his bark was worse than his bite. David acted immediately. He ran *towards* Goliath.

SEVEN DISTINCTIONS OF A TRUE CHAMPION

In a moment, a paralyzed, frightened band of men transformed into a courageous army because one teenage boy's spine stiffened. How did David defeat Goliath?

1. His *view* of Goliath was different. He didn't see a giant. He saw a huge man cursing God.

2. His *motives* were different. David was not after victory to soothe his ego; it was to bring honor and glory to God.

3. His *exposure* differed from others. Others had made a reputation on the public battlefield; David privately perfected his skills with an invisible audience.

4. He used proven *methods*. David perfected his methods before they were needed in battle. His diligence made him a marksman with the slingshot.

5. His *attitude* was different. David believed and spoke as if God had already given him the victory before he saw it happen.

6. His *trust* was different. He refused to wear King Saul's armor, preferring to trust in what worked for him.

7. His *actions* were different. While the army of God was paralyzed in fear, David ran towards the giant and never let doubt in.

David flung the first stone and it hit the bull's-eye. Goliath fell. David ran towards him, and took Goliath's sword and cut off his head. Capture your position here comparatively with your debts. You don't just kill debt; you must cut off its head. Once you fire debt, with its head cut off, it can never be hired back.

> *Are you ready to defeat your Goliath?*

It is one thing to *want* to be a king. It is a completely different thing to become one. Leadership is contagious. The role of a leader is not part-time, not full time, but all the time. You are not called only to be a leader at work, but also at home, at church, in front of your children, everywhere you go. The title "Leader" is not for what you do at work, it is a description for how you live your life. Since Saul was afraid and weak, God's army was afraid and weak. David changed an army with his abilities.

David led the army of God to victory that day. He became known as a leader that day. You have the same power today as David had the day he defeated Goliath. The question is; do you have the will to defeat your Goliath? Anyone who does what he wants only when it is convenient or he is in the mood is not going to be successful. You never see David making excuses. David was focused on victory and didn't need an alternative plan.

IDENTIFY YOUR GOLIATH AND SLAY HIM

There is a Goliath standing in front of you that is restricting you from obtaining God's financial promises. Maybe your Goliath is fear or lack of self-confidence. Or perhaps it is lack of order or inability to focus. Whatever your Goliath is, you can defeat it. One of the largest giants I have observed in others' lives is they do not have a financial vision. Vision starts from within. It grows based upon your history. David slew a lion and a bear; next came the giant. Then David conquered countries for God and was called in Acts 13:22 "a man after (God's) own heart." Unfulfilled kings become spectators. Imagine King Saul cowering in the corner as David was running towards Goliath. Maybe David's brothers are hollering at him, COME BACK! Unfulfilled kings become spectators in the battles of life. Not only that, they become drop outs. God created you in His image and has given you dominion. Be a participator and not a spectator in your finances.

WOMEN – THE NEXT WAVE OF LEADERS

I have found that women have taken the dominant role in managing the family finances. Over 80% of the spending plans I create for couples involve the wife being the money manager in the household. This is OK, but husbands, this doesn't give you the right to sit on the sidelines and only

> *God expects financial responsibility from His sons and His daughters.*

get involved in the families' finances when you want to. You have to be a participant. Since 1984, the number of women in graduate school has exceeded the number of men. 95% of family financial decisions are made by women and women business owners employ more than 35% more employees than all the Fortune 500 employees combined. With women starting more than 400 new businesses each day (more than twice as many as men do) these statistics show us that God is no respecter of persons. The days of women being considered unfit to handle their money are long gone. God expects financial responsibility from His sons *and* His daughters.

NO BATTLES, NO VICTORIES

Everything we do is a process. Whether it is raising our children, being a good spouse, being a good employee, being a good employer, God is giving the Kings a process to always be prepared for the battle. Goliath had brothers. Just because you kill one Goliath, doesn't mean others aren't waiting to stand in your way. The first Goliath is the hardest to kill. Now you can always draw upon your victories to defeat all your Goliaths. God never said we would not have battles. He *did* say, "No weapon formed against you will prosper." You will never achieve a great victory without winning a great battle. We weren't created just to get by. You are a winner; you do have leadership abilities to fire debt and hire wealth.

> *You'll never achieve a great victory without winning a great battle.*

There is no time left for excuses. Today is the first day of the rest of your life. You might be saying, I have no financial skills. Or maybe you're thinking, I don't know how to save and invest. Perhaps you know the right thing to do but procrastinate in taking action. Take responsibility for your future. Be like Isaiah in 6:8 when he said, "Here I am God, send me." It's time for you to become like David and run towards your debt to slay it.

At Disney World in Orlando, Florida, the GE carousel has a song that sticks in my head all day long when I visit that attraction. It begins with "Now is the time, now is the best time of your life…" I hope you feel the same way as this song declares. This is the best time of your financial life when you walk towards the plans that God has for you, daily!

Greg Petsch
Magnolia, TX
March, 2006

END NOTES

INTRODUCTION

1. At the time of this writing, the typical household in America has net assets of $93,100, mostly in home equity (Federal Reserve Triennial Survey released February 2006).

2. Federal Reserve data-based economic analysis commissioned by the Consumer Federation of America (CFA) and DirectAdvice; Washington, D.C., April 26, 2000.

3. In March 2000 the NASDAQ peaked at over 5,047 and today it is around 2,300. It still has yet to recover like the DOW and the S&P have. The NASDAQ must increase 119% just to get back where it was when this article was written.

4. "Retirement Insecurity: The Income Shortfalls Awaiting the Soon-to-Retire," (Edward N. Wolff, May 2002)

5. A related CFA/DirectAdvice public opinion survey. (DirectAdvice, PRNewswire April 26)

6. "Workers Have Retirement Overconfidence" Associate Press, April 4, 2006 by Eileen Alt Powell

CHAPTER 1

1. Google Data (April 12, 2006)

2. It is estimated that only 2% of Americans who have fired debt and live totally debt free including their home. www.newstepsolutions.com/debt statistics web site

CHAPTER 2

1. America now exceeds $12.4 trillion dollars in output. How blessed are we? The world's total GDP is estimated to be $59.38 trillion. Therefore, America represents over 20% of the total GDP in the world. Federal Reserve data-based economic analysis commissioned by the Consumer Federation of America (CFA) and DirectAdvice. www.cia.gov/cia/publications/factbook/rankorder/2001rank.html

2. For the 2007 budget, President Bush submitted a spending plan for $2.77 trillion and income of $2.41 trillion, a planned shortage of $354 billion. (Chicago Tribune, Bush '07 budget not expected to erase much of U.S. red ink. February 7, 2006)

3. When you add all the debt of the above sectors and add the state and local government debt, it totals more than *$44 trillion*. As a percentage of our GDP it is 355%. Business sector debt, Financial sector debt and Household debt totals included in this web site. www.mwhodges.home.att.net/nat-debt/debt-nat-a.htm

4. www.generousgiving.org.

CHAPTER 3

1. www.generousgiving.org

2. www.generousgiving.org

3. www.generousgiving.org

4. More than 43% of American families routinely spend more than they earn. www.newstepsolutions.com/debt-statistics.htm

5. Last year America recorded the largest number of bankruptcies in the world – more than two million. (Personal Bankruptcies in 2005 by Flexo, January 11, 2006)

CHAPTER 4

1. More than 43% of American families routinely spend more than they earn. www.newstepsolutions.com/debt-statistics.htm

CHAPTER 5

1. One statistic says that people generally earn within 20 percent of the people in their immediate circle of friends. (ATTRIBUTION)

2. Percent of people tithing www.generousgiving.org

3. Dr. C. Thomas Anderson, in his book, *Becoming a Millionaire God's Way.*

CHAPTER 6

1. More than half of all Americans have no retirement savings. (Kiplinger's Personal Finance, January 2001)

2. 60% of workers say they are behind schedule when it comes to planning and saving for retirement (2001 Retirement Confidence Survey)

3. Over the past 50 years, the Standard & Poor's 500 stock has averaged 10.4% total return per year. Inflation over the same 50 year period has averaged 4/1%. Thus, stocks have produced a real rate of return of 6.3% per year over the past 50 years. (BTN Research, Department of Labor, February 13, 2006)

4. More than 25% of the total workforce in the United States will reach retirement age by 2010. (What happens when the baby boomer bubble burst, June 22, 2005)

5. 62% of retirees will retire with less than $10,000 income per year. (U.S. Census Bureau)

CHAPTER 7

1. Although the life expectancy from birth for all people in the United States is 77.7 years, those who live to age 65 will have an average of almost 18 additional years left to live, making their life expectancy almost 83 years. www.geography.about.com

2. In 2005, economists reported America had a negative savings rate. (How long can Americans sustain a negative savings rate, John Waggoner, USA Today March 1, 2006)

3. Student loan debt increased by 55 percent among recent graduates of private four-year colleges with student loan debt. These graduates owed an average of $16,500 in 1999/2000, compared to $10,600 in 1989/1990 (all figures in 2002 dollars). *The Debt Explosion Among College Graduates* by Heather Boushey April 3, 2003.

4. High school graduates earn an average of $1.2 million over their working life. (According to the Census Bureau)

5. Associate's degree holders earn about $1.6 million; and bachelor's degree holders earn about $2.1 million. (Day and Newburger, 2002).

6. Nearly 70% of pre-retirees report they plan to work part time or never retire at all. (AARP Research)

7. Unfortunately, for more than half of soon to be retirees social security represents over half of their income source. www.ncpssm.org/pdf/MiddleClassReliance.pdf
May 18, 2005

8. Data between 1991 and 2005 for the return on investment for Large Cap Growth companies return an average 9.89%, core bonds returned 7.28% and high yield bonds returned 10.39%. (Principle Financial Group, 2006)

9. If you spend $3,000 a month in 2006, at 4.1% average annual inflation, you will need $6,701 in 2026 to have the same purchasing power that $3,000 does today. (Greg Petsch retirement planning program, April 2006)

CHAPTER 8

1. Seven distinctions of a true champion. (paraphrased from John C. Maxwell, John Maxwell Leadership Bible, p. 342)

2. Since 1984, the number of women in graduate school has exceeded the number of men. 95% of family financial decisions are made by women and women business owners employ more than 35% more employees than all the Fortune 500 employees combined. www.stopharass.com/article-women-marketplace.htm

GREG E. PETSCH

Greg E. Petsch is the former Senior Vice President for Manufacturing and Quality for Compaq Computer Corporation in Houston, TX. While at Compaq, Greg was responsible for $1 billion a year operating budget, and purchased material totaling $25 billion. He oversaw manufacturing plants in Houston, Scotland, Singapore, China, Taiwan and Brazil.

Greg was named the Director of the Financial Ministry at Lakewood Church in Houston, Texas, currently the largest church in America. Greg has traveled extensively across America, to London, the Dominican Republic, Rwanda, Africa, Guatemala and Germany teaching people how to break the bondage of debt.

Greg E. Petsch is a member of the Board of Directors for Administaff (ASF), a professional employment organization (www.Administaff.com)